A MEDLEY *of* RECIPES

Steamboat Seasons

Celebrating the Flavors of Steamboat Springs with the

Guild of Strings in the Mountains Music Festival

Steamboat Seasons

Published by Strings in the Mountains Music Festival
Copyright © 2005 by Strings in the Mountains Music Festival
P.O. Box 774627
Steamboat Springs, Colorado 80477

Library of Congress Control Number: 2005900442
ISBN: 0-9765390-0-4

Edited, Designed, and Manufactured by
Favorite Recipes® Press
an imprint of

FRP

P.O. Box 305142
Nashville, Tennessee 37230
800-358-0560

Art Director: Steve Newman
Book Design: David Malone
Project Manager: Tanis Westbrook

Printed in China
First Printing: 2005
12,500 copies

Photography: pages 8, 11, 172 Copyright © by Corey Kopischke, www.coreykopischke.com
Photography: pages 60, 63, 108, 111, 175 Copyright © by Chris Selby

Symbolizes a note about the recipe.

Symbolizes an altitude alert.

Symbolizes recipes that can be prepared ahead.

All recipes have been tested at Steamboat Springs' elevation of 7,000 feet.
The altitude alert tells what changes are needed for sea level. Some general altitude rules are:

Sea-level cooking times are shorter, and more leavening is needed in baked goods.

The size and quantity of eggs in cakes, muffins, or brownies is important at altitude to keep the cake from falling.

Water boils at 199 degrees in Steamboat Springs, resulting in slower cooking.
When a range of time is given, choose the shorter for sea level. For meats, be sure to check the temperature with an instant-read thermometer to avoid undercooking or overcooking.

Thanks

The Cookbook Committee

Chairperson
Kathy Vaynkof

Core Team
Dasha Durian　•　Marsha Grant　•　Tina Greig　•　Tibby Speare

Section or Function Leaders
Liz Aldendifer　•　Sandy Berger　•　Jane Carpenter　•　Dasha Durian
Marsha Grant　•　Barbara Hilf　•　Charlotte Jensen
Elaine Love　•　Lois McKown
Suzi Mitchell　•　Gail Overgaard　•　Marit Perkins

Photography
Corey Kopischke & Chris Selby

Art
Julie Anderson　•　Robert Dieckhoff　•　Edie Dismuke　•　David Taylor

Special Thanks
Strings in the Mountains Staff
Strings in the Mountains Board of Directors
Kitchen Tour Committee and Participants
Riley Polumbus

The mission of Strings in the Mountains Music Festival is to present diverse programming of fine music
with an emphasis on chamber music, in an intimate and friendly setting, fostering an appreciation for music
and stimulating the cultural, educational, and economic environment of the community.
The Guild of Strings in the Mountains Music Festival supports the above mission through year-round
volunteer support, financial support, and acting as the integrating body between the festival and the community.
The proceeds from the sale of Steamboat Seasons will be used to support the Strings mission.

Foreword

Steamboat Springs has been my home for over twenty years, and Strings

in the Mountains has been one of the important reasons for the passion

I have for this gorgeous place.

My job as a sports broadcaster dictates that I must travel quite a bit. It's then

that I most miss the music, beauty, and food that so enhance the experience

of living here.

The Guild of Strings in the Mountains has created a cookbook that seems to

me to be a natural extension of the celebration that is Steamboat Springs.

I know that you'll enjoy it. It will allow you to almost literally enjoy a "taste"

of Strings and Steamboat.

Verne Lundquist

CBS Sports

Table of Contents

Introduction

Take a magnificent mountain valley; add high blue skies, warm days, and cool nights; and

mix in the pioneering spirit and a zest for life. The end result is the inspiration for and

the creation of Strings in the Mountains Music Festival in Steamboat Springs, Colorado.

From a modest beginning in 1988 to its permanent home at Music Festival Park in

2004, Strings in the Mountains Music Festival has come of age. Founders Kay Clagett

and Betse Grassby have orchestrated the growth of this award-winning festival from a

few summer concerts to one that now presents more than eighty events each year.

While chamber music remains at the heart of the festival, the diverse programming

includes the "Different Tempo" series, featuring the best in jazz, country, pops, world, and

bluegrass, plus the "Imagine That" programs designed for youth and family audiences.

The Guild of Strings in the Mountains began in 1990 to act as an integrating group

between the festival and the community. Throughout the years, the Guild has held

many fund-raising events involving food, so it seemed a natural progression to create

this cookbook. With *Steamboat Seasons*, we invite you to share our love of cooking,

our passion for music, and the flavor of our unique mountain community.

A Little Piece of Heaven

"Of all the venues and festivals one could play, I cannot imagine there being a better event than Strings. For five consecutive years, I have been honored and blessed to be part of what I consider to be one of the premier musical events anywhere. The integrity of the staff, the venue, and the audience is unsurpassed, and for that and every other reason, it's my desire to be a part of it forever."

Brent Rowan, Academy of Country Music's 2004 Guitarist of the Year

80477

Lately I've been thinkin' 'bout when our time is done
The odds and probabilities ahead for everyone
Now I don't know for certain what the next life has in store
But as for me and this one, I could never ask for more.

I've never walked on streets of gold or seen a crystal sea
But I cannot imagine something prettier to me
Than a Yampa Valley Sunset, or the flattops in the fall
And a full moon night on Buffalo Pass just about says it all.

So if St. Peter seems too busy to let some new folks in
I think I'll just turn around and come right back again
Cause in northern Colorado, there's a little piece of heaven
Known by those who live there as 80477.

If home is where your heart is, then mine is surely here
Where yesterday is cloudy, and forever seems so clear
When you look around and add it up, life could be much worse
And I'm proud to be a victim of the Yampa Valley Curse.

So if St. Peter seems too busy to let some new folks in
I think I'll just turn around and come right back again
Cause in northern Colorado, there's a little piece of heaven
Known by those who live there as 80477.

Words and Music by: Brent Rowan

©2001 Wing And A Prayer Music Co., Inc. (ASCAP)

P.O. Box 120665

Nashville, Tennessee 37212

All Rights Reserved. International Copyright Secured. Used by Permission.

This and other music available at http://www.brentrowan.com

Summer

Sagebrush and mule's ears envelop the landscape of Sleeping Giant.

PHOTOGRAPH BY COREY KOPISCHKE

Grilling

Shrimp Ceviche with Tortilla Chips
16

Cucumber & Yogurt Soup
19

Herbed Pork Tenderloin
31

Tortellini Greek Salad
21

Grilled Vegetable Salad
22

Fresh Peach Pie
55

Rainbow Weekend Brunch

Scotch Eggs
16

Wine & Cheese Strata
46

Smoked Duck Hash
44

Breakfast Cookies
50

Fruit Platter

Columbine and violet asters surround Dumont Lake at Rabbit Ears Pass.

PHOTOGRAPH BY COREY KOPISCHKE

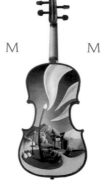

Contemplations

This elixir is the perfect beginning to an introspective evening.

MUSICIAN LAMBERT ORKIS

2 egg whites
1 1/4 ounces freshly squeezed lemon juice
3/4 ounce Chambord liqueur (or more, according to taste)
5 ounces premium vodka (100 proof preferred), kept in freezer 24 hours
5 large ice cubes, crushed (spring water preferred)

1. Chill 2 sherbet or Champagne glasses in the freezer for 4 hours.
2. Mix the egg whites and lemon juice in a blender running at the highest speed.
3. With the blender running, add the Chambord and vodka.
4. Stop the blender, add the crushed ice, and blend on low for about 15 seconds or until the mixture is cold.
5. Strain into the chilled glasses.

Prep Time: 10 minutes   Chill Time: 24 hours   Yield: 2 stupendous drinks

Gorgonzola & Macadamia Spread

Rich and buttery.

2 packages (8 ounces each) cream cheese, softened
8 ounces Gorgonzola cheese, softened
1/2 cup (1 stick) butter, softened
1 cup ground macadamia nuts
1 cup chopped parsley
Plain crackers

1. Blend the cheeses and butter in a bowl.
2. Layer the cheese mixture, ground nuts and parsley 1/2 at a time on a serving platter.
3. Let the flavors blend for several hours.
4. Serve at room temperature with plain crackers.

Prep Time: 20 minutes   Set Time: 2 hours   Yield: 10 to 12 servings

Lambert Orkis is the principal keyboardist for the National Symphony Orchestra. He has garnered international recognition for his performances and recordings of contemporary music, as well as classical chamber music. Mr. Orkis has collaborated with some of the world's great artists and has appeared worldwide with violinist Anne-Sophie Mutter.

Walnut Corn Spread

A creamy spread with lively flavors.

1 package (8 ounces) cream
  cheese, softened
1 tablespoon cumin
1/8 teaspoon cayenne pepper,
  or to taste
1/4 cup fresh lime juice
1 teaspoon salt
Freshly ground black pepper
Dash of lemon pepper

Dash of Tabasco sauce
1 can (8 ounces) whole
  yellow corn, drained
1 cup chopped walnuts,
  toasted
1 can (4 ounces) diced
  green chiles
3 green onions, chopped
Tortilla chips or flour tortillas

1. Whip the cream cheese in a large bowl with an electric mixer until fluffy.
2. Beat in the cumin, cayenne pepper, lime juice, salt, black pepper, lemon pepper and Tabasco sauce. Stir in the corn, walnuts, green chiles and green onions.
3. Chill at least 8 hours before serving.
4. Can be served with tortilla chips or spread on flour tortillas, rolled tightly, and sliced into 1/2-inch pieces.

Prep Time: 15 minutes   Chill Time: 8+ hours   Yield: 3 1/2 cups

Italian Tomatoes & Feta

Make ahead and bake just before company arrives.

1 teaspoon lemon juice
1/4 teaspoon crushed red
  pepper flakes
1 can (14 1/2 ounces) diced
  Italian tomatoes with basil,
  garlic and oregano, drained

2 garlic cloves, minced
4 ounces feta cheese,
  crumbled
32 (1/2-inch-thick) slices
  French bread, toasted, or
  pita triangles, toasted

1. Preheat the oven to 350 degrees. Spray a shallow 1-quart baking dish with nonstick cooking spray.
2. Combine the lemon juice, red pepper flakes, tomatoes and garlic in a bowl.
3. Sprinkle the cheese in the baking dish. Top with the tomato mixture.
4. Bake for 20 minutes.
5. Serve with lightly toasted French bread or toasted pita triangles.

Prep Time: 10 minutes   Cook Time: 20 minutes   Yield: 16 servings

Sea Scallops with Avocado Corn Salsa

Gently grilled scallops top a fresh and colorful salsa.

1 tablespoon olive oil
12 sea scallops
Salt and freshly ground pepper to taste
1/8 teaspoon chili powder or favorite seasoning spice mix
2 avocados, diced
1 cup roasted or frozen corn kernels
3 tablespoons diced onion
1 jalapeño chile, seeded and diced
2 tablespoons chopped cilantro
1 tablespoon lime juice
2 tablespoons sour cream
1/2 cup finely diced red bell pepper
Fried or baked flour tortillas, cut into quarters (optional)

1. Preheat the grill.
2. Lightly oil the scallops and season with salt, pepper and chili powder. Set aside.
3. Combine the avocados, corn kernels, onion, jalapeño chile, cilantro, lime juice, sour cream, salt and pepper. Set aside.
4. Grill the scallops until done, about 2 minutes per side. Do not overcook.
5. Divide the avocado mixture among 4 small plates and top each with 3 scallops. Sprinkle with the bell pepper and serve with tortilla pieces.

Prep Time: 20 minutes   Cook Time: 4 minutes

Yield: 4 first-course servings

The heart of the Strings in the Mountains Music Festival is the Chamber Music and Chamber Orchestra series. Directed by husband and wife team Katherine Collier and Yizak Schotten, these musical offerings feature an exciting repertoire performed by internationally renowned artists. For music lovers with slightly different tastes, the Different Tempo series features the best in contemporary jazz, country, and big band music. The high caliber of all the Strings' offerings has made Steamboat Springs a summer cultural destination.

To hard-cook eggs, place eggs in a single layer in a saucepan. Cover with water and bring to a simmer. Reduce the heat to a slow simmer and cook for fifteen minutes. Drain and then cover with cold water.

Shrimp Ceviche

Dynamite flavor makes this a much sought after starter.

$^1/_2$ cup chopped onion
6 cups water
1 pound medium shrimp
$^1/_2$ cup fresh lime juice
1 cup peeled, seeded and
   chopped cucumber
2 tablespoons Mexican
   hot sauce

$^1/_2$ cup ketchup
1 tablespoon to $^1/_3$ cup
   chopped fresh cilantro, or
   to taste
1 tablespoon vegetable oil
$^1/_4$ teaspoon salt
Tortilla chips

1. Place the chopped onion in a sieve. Rinse with cold water and drain well.
2. Bring 6 cups water to a boil in a saucepan. Add the shrimp and cook for 3 minutes or until done. Rinse the shrimp with cold water and let cool. Peel, devein and chop the shrimp.
3. Combine the shrimp and lime juice in a large bowl. Cover and chill for 1 hour.
4. Drain the shrimp. Stir in the onion, cucumber, hot sauce, ketchup, cilantro, oil and salt. Serve chilled with tortilla chips.

Prep Time: 25 minutes   Chill Time: 1 hour   Cook Time: 3 minutes

Yield: 3 cups

Scotch Eggs

These baked sausage-covered hard-cooked eggs can be served as appetizers or for brunch and also travel well for hikes or picnics.

1 pound low-fat sausage
4 eggs, hard-cooked, rinsed
   and dried

$^1/_4$ cup dried bread crumbs
$^1/_4$ cup (1 ounce) finely
   grated Parmesan cheese

1. Preheat the oven to 400 degrees. Grease a 9-inch pie plate or a 9x11-inch baking dish, large enough to hold the covered eggs without touching each other.
2. Divide the sausage into 4 patties. With wet hands, mold each patty evenly around an egg, being careful to completely cover the egg and squeezing out any air that may become trapped between the egg and the sausage.
3. Mix the bread crumbs and cheese in a shallow dish. Roll each sausage-covered egg in the crumb mixture until completely covered. Place in the pie plate.
4. Bake for 30 minutes, turning once. Serve warm or chilled.

Prep Time: 18 minutes   Cook Time: 30 minutes   Yield: 24 appetizer pieces

Roasted Corn Soup

Made with fresh, sweet Colorado corn complemented by a dynamite sauce.

SOUP

3 ears corn, shucked

1 tablespoon butter

1/2 onion, finely diced

2 to 3 garlic cloves, minced

1 cup dry white wine

2 1/2 cups chicken stock or vegetable stock

1 cup heavy cream or half-and-half

Salt and freshly ground pepper to taste

SMOKED CHILE CREAM

1/2 cup sour cream

1 to 2 teaspoons seeded chopped chipotle chiles
   in adobo sauce

1 teaspoon fresh lime juice

Salt and freshly ground pepper to taste

Fresh marjoram or chopped chives for garnish

FOR THE SOUP:

1. Roast the corn on a grill rack over medium heat for about 8 to 10 minutes, rotating every few minutes. Set aside to cool. Cut the kernels off the cob.
2. Melt the butter in a large saucepan. Sauté the onion and garlic in the butter for about 4 minutes or until translucent.
3. Add the corn kernels and wine. Simmer for 10 to 12 minutes or until the wine is almost evaporated.
4. Add the stock and bring to a boil. Reduce the heat and simmer for about 10 minutes.
5. Add the cream and cook for about 15 minutes or until the soup has thickened slightly.
6. Purée half the soup in a food processor. Return to the saucepan and add salt and pepper.

FOR THE SMOKED CHILE CREAM:

1. Combine the sour cream, chipotle chiles, lime juice, salt and pepper and push through a sieve.
2. Serve the soup hot with the Chile Cream. Garnish with fresh herbs.

Prep Time: 20 minutes   Cook Time: 40 minutes   Yield: 4 to 6 servings

For a few weeks each summer, Coloradoans are blessed with some of the best corn in the world. Olathe Sweet from the western slope town of Olathe is bred to maintain its sugar level; it is hand-picked and immersed in icy cold water to protect its tender kernels and succulent flavor. Choose plump ears that are tapered to immature kernels and refrigerate. Cook no more than 60 seconds in boiling water or roast on the grill.

Chicken Enchilada Soup

The Old West Steakhouse provides fine dining in a relaxed Western atmosphere.
It has been located in historic downtown Steamboat since the 1970s.

DON SILVA

2 to 3 pounds chicken breasts
$^1/_2$ cup diced red bell pepper
$^1/_2$ cup diced green bell
  pepper
$^1/_2$ cup diced yellow onion
$^1/_4$ cup diced green onions
$^1/_4$ cup butter
2 cups salsa
1 can (16 ounces) red
  enchilada sauce
$^1/_2$ cup sliced black olives
2 tablespoons cumin

$1^1/_2$ tablespoons chili
  powder
1 tablespoon sugar
2 cups heavy cream
2 cups half-and-half
2 tablespoons butter,
  softened
2 tablespoons flour
3 cups shredded Monterey
  Jack cheese
3 cups shredded sharp
  Cheddar cheese

1. Cook the chicken in 6 cups boiling water in a stockpot for about 20 to 30 minutes or until cooked through. Remove the chicken and cut into $^3/_8$-inch pieces. Return the chicken to the water.
2. Sauté the bell peppers, onion and green onions in $^1/_4$ cup butter in a skillet. Add to the stockpot.
3. Add the salsa, enchilada sauce, olives, cumin, chili powder and sugar. Bring to a boil and simmer for 15 to 20 minutes.
4. Add the cream and half-and-half. Return to a boil.
5. Combine 2 tablespoons butter and the flour, stirring to incorporate. Add to the soup and simmer for 15 to 20 minutes.
6. Add the cheeses gradually, stirring until melted and blended into the soup.

Prep Time: 30 minutes   Cook Time: 1 hour 15 minutes   Yield: 8 to 10 servings

Cucumber & Yogurt Soup

Delight in this Persian staple, the refreshing "Soupe Mast va Kkair."

1/2 cup raisins
2 to 3 cups yogurt (nonfat is OK)
1/2 cup light cream (milk is OK)
1 egg, hard-cooked and chopped (optional)
6 ice cubes
1 cucumber, peeled, seeded and chopped
1/4 cup chopped green onions
2 teaspoons salt
1/2 teaspoon freshly ground pepper
1 cup cold water
1 tablespoon finely minced parsley
1 tablespoon finely minced fresh dill, or
    1 teaspoon dried dill weed

1. Soak the raisins in cold water for 5 minutes.
2. Place the yogurt in a large bowl. Add the cream, egg, ice cubes, cucumber, green onions, salt and pepper.
3. Drain the raisins and add to the yogurt mixture.
4. Add 1 cup water and mix well.
5. Refrigerate for 2 to 3 hours or up to 1 day.
6. Serve garnished with parsley and dill.

Prep Time: 15 minutes   Chill Time: 2 to 3 hours   Yield: 4 to 5 servings

Yogurt dates back to ancient times. A very valuable food, it is high in protein and calcium, aids in digestion, and helps with the manufacture of vitamin B. The healthy bacteria in yogurt are destroyed by heat, so add to foods after cooking.

Gazpacho

*This recipe from Blue Bonnet Catering utilizes the blender
to impart more flavor and add body.*

CHEF MELISSA CARTAN

$1/4$ red onion
1 English cucumber, peeled and chopped, divided
1 large red bell pepper, chopped, divided
$1/4$ cup balsamic vinegar
1 tablespoon chopped garlic
2 large cans (28 ounces each) diced tomatoes with juice
4 ribs celery, chopped
$1/2$ teaspoon salt, or to taste
$1/2$ teaspoon freshly ground black pepper
Pinch of red pepper flakes
Avocado slices and sour cream for garnish

1. Process the red onion, $1/2$ of the cucumber, $1/2$ of the bell pepper, balsamic vinegar, garlic and 1 can of the tomatoes in a blender on high speed until completely mixed.
2. Combine the remaining cucumber, remaining bell pepper, celery, remaining 1 can tomatoes, salt, black pepper and red pepper flakes in a mixing bowl. Add the blended mixture.
3. Chill for at least 4 hours or up to 2 days.
4. Garnish each serving with an avocado slice and a dollop of sour cream.

Prep Time: 20 to 25 minutes   Chill Time: 4 hours   Yield: 8 to 12 servings

Arugula, Fennel, & Avocado Salad

Feisty arugula combines with the crisp fennel and smooth avocados.

6 cups (4 ounces) baby arugula
4 cups (2 small) thinly sliced fennel bulbs,
    lacy tops discarded
2 avocados, sliced
1/3 cup fresh lemon juice
1 tablespoon olive oil
1/2 teaspoon salt
2 tablespoons shaved Parmesan cheese

1. Combine the arugula, fennel, avocado, lemon juice, olive oil and salt in a bowl. Toss gently to coat.
2. Sprinkle the salad mixture with the cheese.

Prep Time: 20 minutes   Yield: 8 servings

Tortellini Greek Salad

Always a hit at summer picnics or potlucks.

2 packages (12 ounces each) tortellini, fresh or frozen, prepared using the package directions
1 can (12 ounces) artichoke hearts, drained and quartered
1 cup diced fresh tomato
1 cup (4 ounces) coarsely crumbled feta cheese
1/2 cup sliced kalamata olives
1/4 cup white wine vinegar
1/4 cup chopped green onions
3 medium garlic cloves, minced
1 tablespoon basil
1/2 cup extra-virgin olive oil
1/2 cup walnuts, toasted and chopped

1. Drain the tortellini and remove to a large serving bowl.
2. Add the artichokes, tomato, cheese and olives.
3. Whisk the vinegar, green onions, garlic and basil in a small bowl. Add the olive oil slowly, whisking until thoroughly combined.
4. Pour the dressing over the tortellini mixture and toss to coat well. Add the walnuts just before serving at room temperature.

Prep Time: 25 minutes   Yield: 3 quarts or 16 (1/2 cup) servings

A tropical root vegetable resembling a giant turnip, the jicama's texture and taste are a cross between a water chestnut and an apple. It is sweet in flavor and can be eaten raw or cooked. Fresh jicama should be smooth and free of blemishes. One pound jicama yields about three cups chopped.

Grilled Vegetable Salad

A *healthy and hearty vegetation salad*

8 cups mixed salad greens, rinsed, cut and spun
16 spears fresh asparagus, trimmed
1 portobello mushroom, stem removed
8 (^{1}/2-inch-thick) slices peeled jicama
4 (^{1}/2-inch-thick) slices eggplant
4 (^{1}/2-inch-thick) slices fennel bulb
4 (^{1}/2-inch-thick) slices sweet or red onion
^{1}/2 red, yellow and/or green bell pepper, seeded
Vinaigrette of choice
Salt and freshly ground pepper to taste
Grated Parmesan cheese (optional)
Tortilla strips

1. Prepare mixed greens and refrigerate.
2. Place all the vegetables in a large shallow dish and add enough vinaigrette to coat each one. Season with salt and pepper. Marinate for 30 minutes.
3. Preheat the grill.
4. Grill the vegetables on a grill rack for 8 to 12 minutes, turning occasionally. The asparagus will be done first; the root vegetables will take longer.
5. Julienne the vegetables.
6. Toss the greens with vinaigrette and sprinkle with Parmesan cheese.
7. Drizzle a small amount of vinaigrette over the vegetables and arrange on top of the salad.
8. Top with tortilla strips and serve.

Prep Time: 15 minutes   Marinate Time: 30 minutes   Cook Time: 8 to 12 minutes

Yield: 4 to 6 servings

Couscous & Garbanzo Bean Salad

Refreshing on a summer's evening, the currants, mint, and pine nuts perk this up.

1 cup quick-cooking couscous
1/4 cup olive oil
1/4 cup fresh lemon juice
1/2 teaspoon minced garlic
1/4 teaspoon cumin
Hot sauce to taste
Salt and freshly ground
   pepper to taste
1 can (15 ounces) garbanzo
   beans, drained and rinsed

1/3 cup dried currants,
   soaked until soft, drained
1/3 cup finely chopped red
   bell pepper
1/4 cup sliced green onions
1/4 cup chopped fresh mint
1/4 cup chopped flat-leaf
   parsley
1/4 cup pine nuts, toasted

Toasting nuts intensifies their flavor. Nuts can be toasted for 3 to 5 minutes in a microwave on High, in a 350-degree oven, or in a skillet over medium heat. Whichever method you choose, watch carefully as nuts can burn quickly.

1. Cook the couscous using the package directions. Let cool.
2. Mix the olive oil, lemon juice, garlic, cumin, hot sauce, salt and pepper in a large bowl. Add the couscous, garbanzo beans, currants, bell pepper, green onions, mint, parsley and pine nuts and stir to mix.
3. Let stand at room temperature for 1 hour or in the refrigerator overnight.

Prep Time: 1 hour   Cool Time: 1 hour or overnight   Yield: 6 cups

Flank Steak Salad

Serve with roasted potatoes, cherry tomatoes, olives, and green beans.

2 pounds flank steak
Olive oil
2 tablespoons sliced shallots
4 to 6 tablespoons capers,
   rinsed
1 1/2 teaspoons lemon juice
1 1/2 tablespoons red wine
   vinegar

1 1/2 tablespoons Dijon
   mustard
1/2 teaspoon salt
1/2 tablespoon cracked pepper
1 cup minced parsley
1 cup cherry tomatoes,
   halved
1/2 cup pitted kalamata olives

1. Rub the flank steak with olive oil. Broil to the desired degree of doneness. Slice the meat thinly and set aside.
2. Combine the shallots, capers, lemon juice, vinegar, Dijon mustard, salt, pepper, parsley, tomatoes and olives in a bowl and mix well.
3. Place the steak in a resealable plastic bag. Pour the marinade over the meat, seal the bag and marinate in the refrigerator overnight.

Prep Time: 10 minutes   Cook Time: 7 to 10 minutes

Marinate Time: Overnight   Yield: 8 servings

Field of Greens

Add variety to mixed field greens with these lively and unusual dressings.

FAT-FREE BLUEBERRY DRESSING
1 cup fresh or frozen blueberries
1 large garlic clove
$^1/_2$ cup balsamic vinegar
1 teaspoon sugar
$^1/_4$ cup water
Salt and freshly ground pepper to taste

1. Combine the blueberries, garlic, vinegar, sugar, water, salt and pepper in a blender and process until smooth.
2. Pour into a glass container and refrigerate until ready to use.

Prep Time: 5 minutes   Yield: 1$^1/_2$ cups

BALSAMIC VINAIGRETTE/MARINADE
4 medium garlic cloves, halved
1$^1/_4$ cups olive oil
$^1/_4$ cup red wine vinegar
$^1/_4$ cup balsamic vinegar
2 teaspoons salt
$^1/_2$ teaspoon freshly ground black or white pepper
$^1/_2$ teaspoon dry mustard
$^1/_4$ cup mayonnaise (optional—use only if creamy dressing desired)

1. Process the garlic in a food processor until finely chopped. Add the olive oil, vinegars, salt, pepper, mustard and mayonnaise. Process for 5 seconds to blend.
2. Refrigerate until ready to use. Bring to room temperature prior to use.

Also makes a great marinade for chicken. Add fresh or dried herbs, such as 2 teaspoons dried oregano (optional). Marinate chicken for 1 to 4 hours in the refrigerator; drain well. Then bake or grill the chicken as usual.

Prep Time: 5 minutes   Yield: 2 cups or 12 servings

PAPAYA SEED DRESSING

$^1/_4$ cup sugar

$^1/_2$ teaspoon dry mustard

2 teaspoons salt

2 tablespoons papaya seeds, rinsed

$^1/_2$ cup tarragon vinegar

$^1/_2$ cup olive oil

2 green onions, finely chopped

1. Combine the sugar, mustard, salt, papaya seeds, vinegar, oil and green onions in a blender and process until smooth.
2. Pour into a glass container and refrigerate until ready to use.

Serving Suggestion: Top greens with sliced avocado, sliced papaya and chopped red onion.

Prep Time: 5 minutes   Yield: 1 cup

PARMESAN DRESSING

$^2/_3$ cup good-quality oil

1 teaspoon salt

$^1/_8$ teaspoon freshly ground pepper

1 tablespoon sugar

Pinch of Italian seasoning

$^1/_3$ cup wine vinegar

2 tablespoons water

$^3/_4$ teaspoon garlic salt

$^1/_4$ teaspoon paprika

$^1/_3$ cup grated Parmesan cheese

1. Combine the oil, salt, pepper, sugar, Italian seasoning, vinegar, water, garlic salt, paprika and Parmesan cheese in a pint jar with a tight-fitting lid.
2. Cover and shake well. Let stand for 30 minutes and shake again.

Serving Suggestion: Top greens with halved grape tomatoes, sliced mushrooms, chunk of green peppers, chopped red onion and shredded Monterey Jack cheese.

Prep Time: 10 minutes   Stand Time: 30 minutes   Yield: 1$^1/_2$ cups

To prepare fresh ginger for a recipe, peel the outer skin with the rounded top of a teaspoon, slice the peeled pieces, smash with the flat side of a knife or cleaver, and mince or grate with a ginger grater. Store the gingerroot in the freezer and grate as needed while still frozen.

Shrimp, Avocado, & Noodle Salad

A light summertime salad with a sparkling ginger dressing.

3 quarts water
³/4 pound large shrimp (about 12), peeled and deveined
4 ounces Asian rice-stick noodles, softened in hot water
   (about 15 minutes)
3 green onions, thinly sliced diagonally
1 large carrot, peeled and cut into julienne strips
Honey Ginger Dressing (see recipe below)
Salt and freshly ground pepper to taste
1 firm avocado

1. Bring the water to a boil in a 4-quart kettle. Add the shrimp and simmer for about 1¹/2 minutes or just until cooked through. Remove the shrimp to a plate with a slotted spoon.
2. Return the water to a boil and add the softened noodles. Cook the noodles for 2 minutes or just until tender.
3. Rinse the noodles in a colander under cold water to stop the cooking process; drain well. Cut the noodles with scissors into 4-inch lengths.
4. Gently toss the shrimp, noodles, onions, carrot and Honey Ginger Dressing in a bowl. Season with salt and pepper.
5. Just before serving, pit and peel the avocado, cut into ¹/2-inch pieces and place on top of the salad.

Prep Time: 20 minutes   Cook Time: 5 minutes   Yield: 2 servings

Honey Ginger Dressing

1 tablespoon honey
1 tablespoon fresh lemon juice
1¹/2 teaspoons peeled minced fresh ginger
2 tablespoons vegetable oil
Salt and freshly ground pepper to taste

1. Whisk together the honey, lemon juice and ginger in a small bowl.
2. Add the oil in a slow stream, whisking until well blended.
3. Season with salt and pepper.

Thai Noodles

Best served at room temperature.

2 tablespoons sugar
1 tablespoon toasted sesame oil
1 tablespoon chili paste
2 tablespoons rice vinegar
2 tablespoons Asian black bean sauce
1 tablespoon fish sauce
1 tablespoon soy sauce
4 ounces rice noodles, cooked and drained
8 ounces fresh bean sprouts
1/2 cup thinly sliced celery
1/2 cup sliced water chestnuts, rinsed
1/2 cup shredded carrots
2 tablespoons sliced green onions
2 tablespoons chopped cilantro
Peanuts

1. Mix the sugar, sesame oil, chili paste, rice vinegar, black bean sauce, fish sauce and soy sauce in a small bowl and set aside.
2. Combine the noodles, bean sprouts, celery, water chestnuts, carrots, green onions and cilantro in a large bowl.
3. Pour the dressing over the noodle mixture and top with peanuts.

♪ For more of a peanut flavor, add 2 or 3 tablespoons of peanut butter to the sauce.

Prep Time: 20 minutes   Cook Time: 5 minutes   Yield: 4 to 6 servings

Once a week during the summer season, visiting musicians and their families are invited to a picnic supper arranged by the Guild and members of the community. Held at private homes, ranches, and parks, these evenings provide the musicians an opportunity to relax and enjoy the fresh mountain air while mingling with colleagues and appreciative guests.

Grilled Beef Tenderloin

The Home Ranch is located in the Elk River Valley at the edge of the Routt National Forest. It is known for its delicious and imaginative food and its combination of European charm and cowboy culture.

CHEF CLYDE NELSON

According to Hugh Carpenter in the book Hot Barbecue, a barbecue mop is any liquid that is brushed on food being grilled or smoked. A mop can be a marinade or a special seasoning combination ranging from a vinegar mix to melted butter, or it can be a barbecue sauce.

3 tablespoons vegetable oil
1 whole beef tenderloin
 (4 to 5 pounds)

DRY RUB
3 tablespoons kosher salt
3 tablespoons coarsely
 ground black pepper
2 tablespoons minced garlic
1 tablespoon paprika
2 teaspoons minced bay leaf
1 1/2 teaspoons cayenne
 pepper

1 1/2 teaspoons dry mustard
1/4 cup chopped fresh parsley

BARBECUE MOP
1 cup beef broth
1/4 cup red wine
1/4 cup Worcestershire sauce
2 tablespoons canola oil
2 serrano or jalapeño chiles,
 crushed
3 tablespoons
 barbecue sauce
Salt and ground black pepper

Oil your hands and rub over the beef.

FOR THE DRY RUB:
1. Combine the salt, pepper, garlic, paprika, bay leaf, cayenne pepper, mustard and parsley in a small bowl.
2. Rub the mixture over the beef. Let stand for 20 to 30 minutes.

FOR THE BARBECUE MOP:
1. Combine the beef broth, wine, Worcestershire sauce, canola oil, chiles, barbecue sauce, salt and pepper in a small bowl.
2. Place the tenderloin over white-hot coals and sear on 1 side for 5 minutes.
3. Brush with mopping sauce. Turn the beef 90 degrees to make criss-cross grill marks and grill for 5 minutes longer.
4. Turn the beef over and grill for 5 minutes longer, continuing to mop every 5 minutes. Turn 2 more times to sear all sides.
5. Move the beef to a cooler part of the grill. Check the internal temperature with an instant-read thermometer. When it reaches 120 degrees, move the beef to the coolest part of the grill and cover loosely with foil.
6. Let stand for 10 to 15 minutes. The temperature should reach 124 to 130 degrees. Medium-rare should be 130 to 135 degrees.

 Sea level may need less cooking time.

Prep Time: 45 minutes   Cook Time: 45 minute   Yield: 10 to 12 servings

Tenderloin Steaks with Salsa Verde

Try this tangy herb salsa the next time you decide to grill steaks. Make the salsa verde in advance so the flavors can blend.

SALSA VERDE
1 cup flat-leaf parsley,
   stems removed
10 large basil leaves
10 large mint leaves
1 tablespoon fresh oregano
1 garlic clove, crushed
1 tablespoon Dijon mustard
1 tablespoon capers, drained
2 anchovy fillets, or
   1 tablespoon anchovy paste
1 teaspoon red wine vinegar

1/2 cup olive oil
Salt and freshly ground
   pepper to taste

STEAKS
1 tablespoon olive oil
1 teaspoon minced garlic
1 teaspoon freshly ground
   pepper
Salt to taste
4 tenderloin fillets
   (6 to 8 ounces each)

FOR THE SALSA VERDE:

1. Purée the parsley, basil, mint, oregano, garlic, Dijon mustard, capers, anchovies and vinegar in a food processor.
2. With the food processor running, add the olive oil in a fine stream.
3. Remove to a small bowl and season with salt and pepper.

FOR THE STEAKS:

1. Combine the olive oil, garlic, pepper and salt and rub on the steaks. Set aside to marinate while the grill is preheating.
2. Grill the steaks for about 5 minutes per side for medium-rare or to desired doneness. Serve with salsa verde.

Serving Suggestion: Serve with grilled corn on the cob.

To grill corn, remove a few of the loose outer husks and trim the silks. Soak the corn in water for a few minutes to keep the husks from drying out too quickly. Place on a grill rack over hot coals and cook for 15 minutes, turning frequently. Remove the husks and serve.

Sea level may need less cooking time.

Prep Time: 15 minutes   Cook Time: 10 minutes   Yield: 4 servings

Flank steak is an extremely lean cut of beef. It is very flavorful but can be tough if overcooked. Marinating, quickly grilling, or broiling over very high heat to medium-rare and then slicing thinly across the grain are the secrets to keeping it tender. Make sure your carving knife is sharp.

Marinated Flank Steak

Fire up the grill for this fast and delicious flank steak flavored with your choice of marinade.

SOY MARINADE
1/4 cup soy sauce
1/4 cup Italian salad dressing
2 teaspoons sugar
1/2 teaspoon ground ginger

RED WINE MARINADE
3/4 cup beef broth
1/4 cup dry red wine

1 tablespoon red wine
   vinegar
2 garlic cloves
1/4 teaspoon hot sauce
1/4 teaspoon salt
Dash of freshly ground
   pepper

1 (1- to 1 1/2-pound) flank
   steak

FOR THE MARINADE:
Combine the soy sauce, salad dressing, sugar and ginger in a small bowl and mix well or place the beef broth, wine, vinegar, garlic, hot sauce, salt and pepper in a blender and blend well.

FOR THE STEAK:
1. Place the steak in a sealable plastic bag. Add the marinade. Seal the bag, being sure the steak is completely coated with marinade. Marinate in the refrigerator for at least 1 hour or up to 8 hours.
2. Preheat the grill to high. Remove the steak from the refrigerator to warm slightly.
3. Place the steak on the grill rack and cook for 3 to 4 minutes per side for medium-rare. Internal temperature should be 130 to 135 degrees. If the steak is cold when it goes on the grill, the cooking time may need to be increased a bit, but don't overcook.
4. Remove from the grill and let stand for 5 minutes. Slice thinly (1/8 to 1/4 inch) across the grain on a sharp bias and serve immediately.
5. If you wish to use any remaining marinade as a sauce, pour into a small saucepan and boil for several minutes.

Serving Suggestion: Serve with grilled vegetables and corn on the cob and never have to heat up the kitchen.

♪ The soy marinade is also good on chicken and any kabob meat.

 Sea level may need less cooking time.

Prep Time: 5 minutes   Marinate Time: 1 to 8 hours
Cook Time: 8 minutes   Yield: 4 servings

Herbed Pork Tenderloin

This very tasty and easy to prepare pork tenderloin is perfect for a casual summer evening on the deck.

1 cup beer or ginger ale
1/2 cup honey
1/2 cup Dijon mustard
1/4 cup vegetable oil
2 teaspoons onion powder
1 1/2 teaspoons crushed rosemary
1 teaspoon garlic powder
1 teaspoon salt
1/4 teaspoon pepper
2 pork tenderloins (1 pound each)
2 tablespoons butter

1. Mix the beer, honey, mustard, oil, onion powder, rosemary, garlic powder, salt and pepper in a bowl. Pour over the tenderloins. Marinate, covered, in the refrigerator overnight.
2. Prepare a charcoal grill or preheat a gas grill to high.
3. Remove the pork from the marinade; reserve the marinade. Grill the pork for 10 minutes per side or until the internal temperature is 145 degrees.
4. Let the pork stand, covered, on a warm plate while you prepare the sauce.
5. Pour the marinade into a medium saucepan and bring to a boil. Boil for several minutes to reduce and thicken. Stir in the butter.
6. Slice the pork and serve with the sauce.

 Sea level may need less cooking time.

Prep Time: 10 minutes   Marinate Time: Overnight   Cook Time: 30 minutes
Yield: 6 to 8 servings

Many locals admit they were lured to Steamboat by the winter but chose to stay for the summer. They are the unwitting victims of the Yampa Valley Curse: "Those who come to the Yampa Valley to live will never be able to leave," proclaimed Ute leader Colorow in 1881. The Ute Indians were among the first visitors, spending their summers here with bountiful hunting and fishing, and relaxing in the soothing natural hot springs. The same expansive natural beauty exists today; each summer, the gorgeous wildflowers are a photographer's dream, and mountain biking, hiking, fishing, horseback riding, and rafting are just a sampling of the summer activities to thrill the outdoor enthusiasts.

Babyback Ribs

Antares provides new world cuisine—an eclectic blend of dishes. It has fireside dining in a historic downtown setting.

CHEF ROCKY LEBRUN

Stop by the Yampa River Botanical Park on Thursdays at noon during the summer season. Music enthusiasts of every age can be found stretched out on the grassy slope with their picnic lunches, enjoying the harmonious blend of music and the beautiful setting. Music on the Green is part of Strings in the Mountains' free summer concerts and is a must for anyone who can spare an hour for a truly wonderful treat.

6 pounds babyback pork ribs
6 ounces hoisin sauce, divided
2 cups packed brown sugar
3 ounces cumin
3 ounces coriander
3 cups chicken broth
1 cup plum sauce
5 serrrano chiles, chopped
Juice and grated zest of 3 oranges
2 tablespoons cornstarch

1. Preheat the oven to 275 degrees.
2. Rub the babyback ribs with 3 ounces of the hoisin sauce. Set aside.
3. Combine the brown sugar, cumin and coriander in a bowl. Pat on the ribs.
4. Bake for 3 to 4 hours or until ribs fold over and break apart.
5. Combine the chicken broth, plum sauce, remaining 3 ounces hoisin sauce, serrano chiles, orange juice and orange zest in a saucepan. Bring to a rolling boil. Reduce the heat to a simmer. Combine the cornstarch and 1/4 cup of the sauce in a mixing cup and stir until smooth. Slowly add the cornstarch mixture to the sauce and cook until thickened.
6. Pour the sauce over the ribs and serve.

Prep Time: 20 minutes   Cook Time: 3 to 4 hours   Yield: 6 servings

Grilled Lamb Chops

Oregano adds a robust flavor to this simple preparation.
Squirt lemon on the chops just before serving.

3 tablespoons oregano
1 teaspoon salt
$^1/_2$ teaspoon freshly ground
   pepper

3 tablespoons red wine
8 lamb loin chops (4 ounces
   each), trimmed
4 garlic cloves, thinly sliced

1. Mix the oregano, salt and pepper in a bowl.
2. Sprinkle the wine over the lamb chops. Pat the spice mixture over the lamb chops and place in a sealable plastic bag. Add the garlic. Seal the bag and refrigerate for 3 hours, turning occasionally.
3. Preheat the grill. Place the lamb chops on a grill rack.
4. Grill the lamb chops for 5 minutes per side or to desired doneness.

Prep Time: 5 minutes   Marinate Time: 3 hours   Cook Time: 10 minutes

Yield: 4 servings

Chicken with Feta & Olives

Quick to prepare and healthy. A nice family dish.

2 tablespoons olive oil
4 boneless skinless chicken
   breasts, cut into strips
1 garlic clove, minced
$^1/_2$ teaspoon oregano
Salt and freshly ground
   pepper to taste
$^1/_4$ cup fresh lemon juice

1 can (14 ounces) diced
   tomatoes
$^1/_2$ teaspoon sugar
12 kalamata olives, pitted
   and halved
$^1/_3$ cup crumbled feta cheese
Hot cooked spaghetti
Chopped fresh parsley

1. Heat the olive oil in a large skillet over medium heat. Add the chicken and brown on all sides.
2. Add the garlic, oregano, salt and pepper. Cook for 2 minutes.
3. Add the lemon juice, undrained tomatoes and sugar.
4. Cover and simmer for 15 minutes.
5. Stir in the olives and cheese.
6. Serve over hot cooked spaghetti. Garnish with parsley.

Prep Time: 10 minutes   Cook Time: 20 minutes   Yield: 4 servings

Diamond Chicken

Named for morels found in Diamond Park near Steamboat, this easy and delectable dish is good with any mushrooms, but if fresh morels come into your life, by all means use them here.

A century ago, Lester Remington came across a startling discovery on his ranch at the foot of Buffalo Pass: a rather large patch of plump strawberries in rows ready for gathering. To this day, no one knows who planted the berries, but Remington sold the crop during what was known as Steamboat's "Strawberry Boom." At its height in 1911, nearly 9,000 crates of strawberries were transported to Denver; eventually, frosts wiped out the fields, but, in the 1930s, the fields blossomed again under the care of Daisy Anderson. Today, the area, including the hot springs, the middle school, and an elementary school, carries the name Strawberry Park, although the patch no longer exists.

2 tablespoons butter or olive oil, or 1 tablespoon each
1 medium onion, chopped
5 garlic cloves
1 pound wild morels, or equivalent amount mixed
   fresh mushrooms
1 chicken (3 pounds), cut up
Salt and freshly ground pepper to taste
2 tablespoons dry white wine or sherry
1/4 cup heavy cream

1. Melt the butter in a large skillet over medium heat. Add the onion, garlic and mushrooms and sauté for 5 minutes.
2. Add the chicken. Cook, covered, for 20 minutes or until the chicken is cooked through. Season with salt and pepper.
3. Add the wine and bring to a boil. Stir in the cream.

♪ This dish is better made a day ahead, adding the cream just before serving.

Prep Time: 15 to 30 minutes   Cook Time: 30 minutes   Yield: 4 servings

Chicken & Yogurt Curry
(Dahi Murgh)

This easy curry is mildly spicy and intoxicating.

1 onion, chopped (about 1½ cups)
3 garlic cloves
1 (1-inch) piece fresh ginger, peeled and grated
½ cup coarsely chopped fresh cilantro leaves and stems
1½ tablespoons vegetable oil
1 teaspoon turmeric
1½ teaspoons garam masala (see recipe on page 43 or
   use store-bought)
1½ teaspoons salt
½ teaspoon cayenne pepper (optional)
½ cup plain yogurt
2 tomatoes, chopped (about 1¾ cups)
1 (3-pound) chicken, cut up
Cilantro for garnish

1. Process the onion, garlic, ginger and ½ cup cilantro in a blender or food processor until a paste forms.
2. Heat the oil in a heavy 3-quart sauté pan. Add the onion mixture and cook over medium heat for about 5 minutes, stirring occasionally.
3. Add the turmeric, garam masala, salt and cayenne pepper. Cook for 1 to 2 minutes longer or until fragrant.
4. Stir in the yogurt and tomatoes. Cook for 1 minute, stirring until well blended.
5. Add the chicken and coat well with the sauce. Cook, covered, over low heat for 30 minutes or until the chicken is cooked through, turning once.
6. Serve with rice and garnish with fresh cilantro.

Prep Time: 25 minutes   Cook Time: 30 to 35 minutes   Yield: 4 to 6 servings

Orange Roughy with Fresh Tomatoes

Using fresh tomatoes adds exceptional flavor to this recipe.
The sauce works well on other types of white fish.

1¹/₃ to 2 pounds orange roughy fillets
Salt and freshly ground pepper
2 tablespoons butter
1 onion, chopped
2 green onions, chopped
1 garlic clove, minced
1¹/₂ tablespoons flour
¹/₂ cup dry white wine
4 tomatoes, peeled, seeded and coarsely chopped
1 tablespoon chopped parsley
Pinch of tarragon
Pinch of thyme
Pinch of basil
¹/₄ cup fine dry bread crumbs
2 tablespoons grated Parmesan cheese

1. Preheat the oven to 350 degrees.
2. Place the fish in a well-buttered baking dish large enough to accommodate the fish in a single layer. Season with salt and pepper.
3. Melt 2 tablespoons butter in a medium saucepan. Add the onion, green onions and garlic and sauté for 5 minutes or until tender but not brown.
4. Stir in the flour. Gradually add the wine, stirring constantly. Bring to a boil and simmer for 5 minutes. Season with salt and pepper.
5. Stir the tomatoes, parsley, tarragon, thyme and basil into the sauce. Pour the sauce over the fish.
6. Sprinkle with the bread crumbs and cheese.
7. Bake for 30 minutes or until the fish flakes easily with a fork.

Prep Time: 30 minutes   Cook Time: 30 minutes   Yield: 3 to 4 servings

Mahi Mahi with Pineapple Salsa

The clean, refreshing flavor of this salsa enhances the richness of the mahi mahi.

FISH
4 mahi mahi fillets (6 to 8 ounces each)
1/2 cup olive oil
2 tablespoons soy sauce
Pinch of pepper
1 tablespoon chopped green onion

PINEAPPLE TOMATILLO SALSA
3 medium tomatillos
2 tablespoons olive oil
1/2 cup diced red onion
1 jalapeño chile, seeded and diced
1 garlic clove, minced
1 1/4 cups diced fresh pineapple
1 1/2 teaspoons lime juice
1 tablespoon chopped cilantro
Salt and pepper to taste

FOR THE FISH:
Place the fish in a large shallow dish or sealable plastic bag. Whisk the olive oil, soy sauce, pepper and green onions in a bowl. Pour over the fish and marinate for no longer than 1 hour.

FOR THE SALSA:
1. While the fish is marinating, preheat the grill and prepare the salsa. Remove the outer papery husk from the tomatillos and rinse well. Rub each with a small amount of the olive oil and grill until slightly blackened and soft. Set aside.
2. Heat the remaining olive oil in a medium skillet. Cook the onion, jalapeño chile and garlic in the hot oil for about 5 minutes or until translucent and soft.
3. Purée the tomatillos and onion mixture in a food processor. Add the pineapple, lime juice and cilantro; pulse quickly to blend. Season with salt and pepper.
4. Remove the fish from the marinade; discard the marinade. Grill for about 3 minutes per side. Top with the salsa.

Prep Time: 45 minutes   Marinate Time: 1 hour   Cook Time: 5 to 6 minutes

Yield: 4 servings

Although not a member of the tomato family, tomatillos look like small green tomatoes with a papery husk. They have a crisp, tart, and distinctive flavor. Available year-round in most supermarkets, they are a good choice for salsas. They store well (up to a month) refrigerated in a paper bag. Choose small, firm, dark green tomatillos. Be sure to rinse them well after removing the husks since they have a sticky surface.

Asian Tuna

The flavor of lime heightens the vibrant Asian marinade.

1 cup light soy sauce
$^1/_3$ cup toasted sesame oil
$^1/_2$ cup fresh lime juice
$^1/_4$ cup mirin
2 tablespoons grated fresh ginger
2 garlic cloves, minced
1 tablespoon red pepper flakes
4 yellowfin tuna steaks, about 1 inch thick
   (6 to 8 ounces each)

1. Combine the soy sauce, sesame oil, lime juice, mirin, ginger, garlic and red pepper flakes in a shallow dish.
2. Place the tuna steaks in a single layer in the soy sauce mixture. Pierce the tuna several times with a fork. Turn the tuna over and marinate for 30 minutes.
3. Preheat a grill and set on high heat.
4. Remove the fish from the marinade, discarding the marinade. Place the fish on a lightly oiled grill rack. Cook for about 3 minutes per side. Remember, they will cook a bit more after being removed from the grill, and this dish is better rare than well done.
5. Serve immediately.

♪ Mirin is a sweetened rice wine used as a seasoning and sweetener, available in the Asian section of most supermarkets.

Prep Time: 5 minutes   Marinate Time: 30 minutes   Cook Time: 6 minutes
Yield: 4 servings

Eggplant Roll-Ups

An unusual presentation of this versatile vegetable.

EGGPLANT ROLLS
1 large eggplant, cut
   lengthwise into
   1/4-inch strips
Canola oil spray
1 carton (16 ounces) nonfat
   ricotta cheese
1 teaspoon basil
1/4 cup (1 ounce) grated
   Parmesan cheese
1/2 teaspoon salt
1/8 teaspoon pepper

SAUCE
1/2 cup chopped onion
3 garlic cloves, minced
1/2 teaspoon thyme
2 tablespoons olive oil
1 can (16 ounces) diced
   tomatoes
Salt and pepper to taste

FOR THE EGGPLANT:

1. Preheat the broiler. Place foil in the bottom of a broiler pan.
2. Place the eggplant in the pan and spray with canola oil. Broil until light brown. Turn the eggplant and repeat.
3. Reduce the oven temperature to 400 degrees. Grease a 7x11-inch baking pan.
4. Mix the ricotta cheese, basil, Parmesan cheese, salt and pepper in a bowl. Place a scoop of the cheese mixture on 1 end of each eggplant strip. Roll the strip around the cheese mixture and place seam side down in the pan.

FOR THE SAUCE:

1. Sauté the onion, garlic and thyme in the olive oil in a saucepan until soft. Add the tomatoes, salt and pepper and simmer for 5 to 10 minutes.
2. Spoon the sauce over the rolls.
3. Bake for 20 to 30 minutes.

Prep Time: 35 minutes   Cook Time: 20 to 30 minutes   Yield: 4 to 6 servings

Mushrooms with Snap Peas

Sugar snap peas are wonderful off the vine if you're lucky enough to have some in your garden.

2 tablespoons olive oil
8 ounces whole mushrooms, cleaned and quartered
2 large green onions, rinsed and cut into 1/4-inch lengths
1 (8-ounce) package sugar snap peas (about 3 cups)
1/4 cup dry sherry
1 teaspoon toasted sesame oil
1 teaspoon toasted sesame seeds for garnish
Salt and freshly ground pepper to taste

1. Heat the olive oil in a 12-inch skillet. Add the mushrooms and green onions and sauté for about 5 to 7 minutes or until the mushrooms are golden brown.
2. Add the snap peas and sherry. Cook for 1 minute. Reduce the heat and cover the skillet.
3. Cook over low heat for 2 to 3 minutes or until the peas are heated through but still crisp.
4. Remove from the heat. Drizzle with the sesame oil and sprinkle with the sesame seeds, salt and pepper.
5. Serve immediately.

Prep Time: 10 minutes   Cook Time: 10 minutes   Yield: 4 servings

Hot Tomatoes

Bacon and tomato are a natural combination. Enjoy them in the baked layers of this scrumptious dish.

4 slices bacon, diced
1 tablespoon olive oil
1 garlic clove, minced
1 onion, thinly sliced
4 ounces mushrooms, sliced
1 tablespoon flour
1/2 teaspoon salt or seasoned salt
5 medium tomatoes, cut into 1/2-inch slices, divided
6 tablespoons grated Parmesan cheese, divided
1 tablespoon butter

1. Fry the bacon in a skillet until crisp. Drain on paper towels, reserving the drippings. (Or cook the bacon in a microwave until crisp and use olive oil instead of drippings.) Crumble the bacon.
2. Sauté the garlic, onion and mushrooms in the reserved drippings in the skillet until tender.
3. Stir in the bacon, flour and salt. Set aside.
4. Preheat the oven to 350 degrees. Grease an 8x8-inch baking dish or spray with nonstick cooking spray.
5. Layer the tomatoes, onion mixture and cheese 1/2 at a time in the baking dish. Dot with the butter.
6. Bake for 25 minutes.

Prep Time: 1/2 hour   Cook Time: 25 minutes   Yield: 6 servings

On the Fourth of July, Strings in the Mountains and the historic Tread of the Pioneers Museum co-host a community concert following the annual downtown parade. The concert stage is conveniently positioned between the food offerings of the Methodist Church's Strawberry Sundae Stand, the Episcopal Church's Hot Dog Grill, and the Museum's Routt Beer Floats. On both sides of the street, people find a viewing spot while children march, dance, and wave their flags as dogs lie patiently in the shade of nearby trees.

Baked Garden Vegetables

Great with roasted or grilled meat or stands on its own as a vegetarian dish.
Vary the vegetables to suit your taste.

1 peeled or unpeeled (8-ounce) potato, finely diced
1 small zucchini, finely diced
1 peeled or unpeeled small eggplant, finely diced
2 green bell peppers, halved and finely diced
2 medium carrots, peeled and sliced
1 small onion, finely diced
$^1/_2$ cup green peas (may use frozen)
2 tablespoons chopped parsley
$1^1/_2$ teaspoons salt
$^3/_4$ teaspoon ground pepper
4 medium tomatoes, sliced
1 cup cooked brown or white rice
    ($^1/_2$ cup uncooked rice = 1 cup cooked)
2 tablespoons red wine vinegar
4 ounces Cheddar cheese, shredded

1. Preheat the oven to 350 degrees. Grease a 9x13-inch baking dish.
2. Mix the potato, zucchini, eggplant, bell peppers, carrots, onion, peas, parsley, salt and pepper in a large bowl.
3. Arrange half the tomato slices in the baking dish. Add layers of half the vegetable mixture, all the rice, remaining vegetable mixture and remaining tomato slices. Sprinkle with the vinegar.
4. Bake, covered with foil, for 1 hour and 45 minutes.
5. Remove the foil and sprinkle with the cheese. Return to the oven and bake, uncovered, until the cheese is melted.

Prep Time: 30 minutes   Cook time: 1 hour 45 minutes   Yield: 6 to 8 servings

Garam Masala

Garam masala is an essential addition to many curries and chutneys.

5 (3-inch) cinnamon sticks
5 tablespoons whole
   cardamom pods (available
   at specialty and health
   food markets)
3 tablespoons whole cloves

$3^{1}/_{2}$ tablespoons whole
   cumin seeds
$1^{1}/_{2}$ tablespoons whole
   coriander seeds
$4^{1}/_{2}$ tablespoons whole black
   peppercorns

1. Heat a dry skillet over medium heat and place all ingredients in the skillet.
2. Cook for 5 to 7 minutes or until aromatic. Be careful not to burn. Remove from the heat and let cool.
3. Separate the cardamom pods from the mixture and place on a cutting board. Using the flat side of a large knife, whack the pods to break them open and remove the seeds. Return the seeds to the spice mixture and discard the pods.
4. Process the spice mixture at high speed in a blender until ground to a fine powder.
5. Store in a dark jar in a cool place. Do not refrigerate. Will keep for 1 to 3 years.

Prep Time: 15 minutes   Cook Time: 7 minutes   Yield: $1^{1}/_{2}$ cups

Peach Chutney

This delicious and beautiful chutney is a wonderful addition to chicken or pork dishes.

5 pounds ripe peaches,
   peeled and thinly sliced
8 large dried chiles
3 cups malt vinegar or
   distilled white vinegar,
   divided
5 garlic cloves

$^{1}/_{2}$ cup chopped peeled
   fresh ginger
$1^{1}/_{2}$ cups sugar
1 cup raisins or sultanas
1 teaspoon garam masala
   (see recipe above)

1. Place the peaches in an 8-quart stockpot.
2. Remove and discard the stalk end and seeds of the chiles. Place the chiles in a shallow bowl and cover with 1 cup of the vinegar. Soak for 10 minutes.
3. Combine the undrained chiles, garlic and ginger in a blender and process at high speed until finely chopped. Add the mixture, remaining 2 cups vinegar, sugar, raisins and garam masala to the peaches and stir to combine.
4. Bring to a boil; reduce the heat. Simmer for 15 minutes.
5. Cool and place in containers for freezing. Also keeps in the refrigerator for a month.

Prep Time: 1 hour 15 minutes   Cook Time: 15 minutes   Yield: $10^{1}/_{2}$ cups

From the fiery hot habanero and its close cousin, the Scotch bonnet, to the moderate jalapeño and poblano, chile peppers add intensity and flavor to the foods we love. Capsaicin is the chemical behind the heat and is present mostly in the seeds and veins. Wear rubber gloves when working with fresh chiles, and don't touch your eyes or sensitive skin. Dried chiles, such as the ancho and chipotle, have a deep and earthy, yet more mellow, flavor.

Smoked Duck Hash

Chef David Nelson is a co-founding partner of the Internet Culinary Portal known as Chef2Chef.net. It is one of the largest culinary sites online.

CHEF DAVID NELSON

1 quart water
3 russet potatoes (about 1 pound), washed and finely diced
4 slices bacon
8 ounces smoked duck breast, cut into 1/8-inch cubes
3 tablespoons finely diced red onion
2 tablespoons finely diced red bell pepper
Salt and freshly ground pepper to taste
8 eggs, cooked over-easy

1. Bring the water to a boil in a saucepan and add the potatoes. Cook for about 7 to 8 minutes or just until tender. Do not overcook or they will fall apart when you brown them later (this can be done the night before). When the potatoes are done, drain well in a strainer.
2. Cook the bacon in a large skillet over medium heat until very crisp. Remove and drain on paper towels. Once cool, chop the bacon into small pieces. Set aside.
3. Cook the duck, onion and bell pepper in the hot bacon drippings in the skillet for 4 to 5 minutes. Add the potatoes and cook for 10 to 15 minutes or until they are brown and begin to get crisp. Season with salt and pepper. Add the bacon and stir.
4. Place a mound of hash in the center of 4 warm plates. Top each with 2 eggs.

♪ This dish may be made with any kind of leftover cooked meat, such as ham, beef, chicken, or turkey. Add other vegetables, if desired.

Prep Time: 15 minutes   Cook Time: 25 minutes   Yield: 4 servings

Southwest Frittata

Great for brunch on the deck or a light supper before a concert.

1 can (4 ounces) diced green chiles, divided
3 corn tortillas, torn into 1-inch pieces, divided
8 ounces (2 cups) shredded Jack cheese
  (or combined Jack/Cheddar), divided
1/2 cup sliced black olives (optional)
4 eggs, beaten
1/3 cup half-and-half or fat-free half-and-half
1/4 teaspoon salt
1/4 teaspoon pepper
1/4 teaspoon cumin
1/4 teaspoon onion salt
1/4 teaspoon garlic salt
1 large tomato, cut into thin wedges
Paprika

1. Spray a 9-inch glass pie plate with nonstick cooking spray.
2. Layer half the green chiles, half the tortilla pieces, half the cheese, all the olives, the remaining green chiles, remaining tortilla pieces and remaining cheese in the pie plate.
3. Mix the eggs, half-and-half, salt, pepper, cumin, onion salt and garlic salt in a bowl with a whisk.
4. Pour the egg mixture evenly over the layers in the pie plate. Place the tomato wedges around the top of the pie on each slice. Sprinkle lightly with paprika.
5. Bake immediately or cover the dish with foil and refrigerate overnight.
6. Preheat the oven to 350 degrees.
7. Bake, uncovered, for 30 minutes (if cooked immediately) or 40 minutes (if chilled overnight), or until set and light brown.
8. Let stand for 10 minutes before slicing.

Prep Time: 15 minutes   Chill Time: Overnight (optional)

Cook Time: 30 to 40 minutes   Yield: 4 servings (6-inch wedges)

Wine & Cheese Strata

Prepared the day before, this is a special breakfast dish.

1/2 large loaf day-old French bread, broken into small pieces
3 tablespoons unsalted butter, melted
4 ounces Monterey Jack cheese, shredded (about 1 cup)
4 ounces Swiss cheese, shredded (about 1 cup)
5 slices Genoa salami, coarsely chopped
8 eggs, beaten
1 1/2 cups milk
1/4 cup dry white wine
2 large green onions, minced
1 1/2 teaspoons Dijon mustard
1/4 teaspoon pepper
3/4 cup sour cream
1/2 cup (2 ounces) grated Parmesan cheese

1. Spray a 9x13-inch 3-quart baking dish with nonstick cooking spray.
2. Place the bread in the baking dish and drizzle with the butter.
3. Sprinkle the Monterey Jack cheese, Swiss cheese and salami over the bread.
4. Combine the eggs, milk, wine, green onions, mustard and pepper and beat until foamy.
5. Pour the egg mixture over the cheese and bread.
6. Cover the dish with foil and refrigerate overnight or up to 24 hours.
7. Remove from the refrigerator 30 minutes before baking.
8. Preheat the oven to 350 degrees.
9. Bake, covered, for about 1 hour or until set.
10. Uncover and spread with the sour cream. Sprinkle with the Parmesan cheese.
11. Bake, uncovered, for about 10 minutes or until crusty and light brown.

For variation, use sausage, chorizo, or smoked salmon instead of salami, top with salsa or marinara sauce, vary the cheese, use Cheddar cheese with ham, or use thinly sliced potatoes or diced cooked potatoes on the bottom instead of the bread.

Prep Time: 20 minutes   Chill Time: Overnight   Cook Time: 1 hour 10 minutes

Yield: 6 servings

Whole Grain Pancakes

Low-fat and full of healthy grains.

MUSICIAN PAUL EACHUS

1 cup whole wheat
    pastry flour
1/2 cup whole wheat flour
1 cup stone-ground cornmeal
1/2 cup wheat bran, oat bran
    or wheat germ
1/2 teaspoon salt
4 teaspoons baking powder
1 teaspoon baking soda
Chopped walnuts or pecans
    (optional)

Ghiradelli chocolate chips to
    taste (optional)
1 teaspoon cinnamon
    (optional)
2 3/4 cups milk (any type)
2 eggs
1/4 cup apple butter or
    applesauce
1 teaspoon vanilla extract

Paul Eachus leads a diverse musical career as conductor, recording engineer, producer, and bass trombonist.

1. Mix the flours, cornmeal, wheat bran, salt, baking powder, baking soda, walnuts, chocolate chips and cinnamon in a large bowl. Set aside.
2. Whisk the milk, eggs, apple butter and vanilla in a medium bowl. Pour into the flour mixture and whisk until smooth.
3. Heat a griddle or skillet to 350 degrees.
4. Pour the batter to make any size pancake. Cook for about 2 1/2 minutes per side, turning when the edges become slightly dry. Serve immediately with maple syrup or Bumbleberry Sauce with yogurt.

Prep Time: 20 minutes   Cook Time: 5 minutes per batch

Yield: 4 to 5 servings, twenty 5-inch pancakes

Bumbleberry Sauce

A good way to use up excess summer berries from your freezer.

2 cups blueberries, rinsed
    (berries can be frozen)
2 cups strawberries, rinsed
    and sliced

2 cups raspberries
1 cup sugar

1. Mix the blueberries, strawberries, raspberries and sugar in a saucepan. Bring to a boil over medium heat, stirring frequently. Reduce the heat and simmer for 15 minutes, stirring occasionally. Cool in the pan.
2. Purée in a blender or food processor and strain through a sieve to remove seeds.
3. Use as desired or freeze for future use. Will keep in the refrigerator for 2 weeks.

Prep Time: 25 minutes   Yield: 3 1/2 cups

Focaccia

Focaccia makes great sandwiches when sliced horizontally.
Also, it can be cut into wedges to dip in olive oil.

1^1/$_2$ cups warm water
1 teaspoon sugar
1 envelope dry yeast
4 cups unbleached all-purpose flour, or
   3 cups all-purpose flour plus 1 cup semolina flour
1 teaspoon salt
^{1}/$_2$ teaspoon oregano or rosemary
^{1}/$_4$ cup olive oil
2 tablespoons olive oil mixed with 1 crushed garlic clove

1. Oil a 9x13-inch baking pan or 2 round 8-inch baking pans.
2. Mix the warm water, sugar and yeast in a small bowl. Let stand for about 5 minutes or until foamy.
3. Measure the flour, salt and oregano into the work bowl of a food processor fitted with a metal blade or a stand mixer with a dough hook.
4. Add the olive oil to the yeast mixture. With the food processor running, pour the yeast mixture into the food processor. Continue processing for about 1 to 2 minutes or until the dough is well mixed and forms a ball.
5. Turn onto the counter and knead a few turns. Place in a greased bowl. Cover and set in a warm place to rise (an electric oven with the light turned on is good) for about 1 hour or until doubled in bulk.
6. Punch the dough down and knead a few turns. Push the dough into the baking pan, trying to fill the entire pan. Brush the top with the oil and garlic mixture. Make a few dimples in the top with your fingers or a chopstick.
7. Set in a warm place to rise for about 45 to 60 minutes or until doubled in bulk.
8. Preheat the oven to 375 degrees.
9. Bake for 20 to 22 minutes or until golden brown.
10. Cool in the pan.

♪ For variation, sprinkle the top with Parmesan cheese before baking, or lay thinly sliced tomatoes on top before baking or finely chop and sauté 1 onion until golden. Let cool before adding to the dough.

♪ Semolina flour, sometimes called "pasta flour," adds a nice flavor. Available at most supermarkets.

Prep Time: 10 minutes   Rise Time: about 2 hours

Cook Time: 20 to 22 minutes   Yield: one 9x13-inch loaf or 2 round loaves

Chocolate Banana Bread

A fun twist on banana bread for chocolate lovers.

1³/4 cups unbleached all-purpose flour
¹/2 cup unsweetened baking cocoa
1 teaspoon baking soda
¹/2 teaspoon salt
¹/2 cup canola oil
1¹/4 cups sugar
1 cup mashed very ripe bananas
   (about 2 bananas)
2 extra-large eggs
1 teaspoon lemon juice or white vinegar
¹/3 cup milk
¹/2 cup chopped walnuts

1. Preheat the oven to 350 degrees. Grease a 5x9-inch loaf pan.
2. Mix the flour, baking cocoa, baking soda and salt in a medium bowl. Set aside.
3. Cream the canola oil and sugar in a large bowl with an electric mixer. Mix in the bananas and eggs.
4. Combine the lemon juice with the milk in a small bowl (it will curdle).
5. Add the flour mixture and milk mixture alternately to the banana mixture. Mix well after each addition. Begin and end with dry ingredients.
6. Stir in the walnuts.
7. Pour into the prepared pan. Bake for about 60 to 65 minutes. Cover loosely with foil for the last 15 minutes to prevent burning the top. The loaf is done when a skewer or toothpick inserted into the center comes out clean or when the bread springs back when lightly touched in the center.
8. Let cool in the pan on a wire rack for at least 30 minutes before turning out of the pan. It is best to cool bread completely before turning out.

Prep Time: 20 minutes   Cook Time: 60 to 65 minutes   Yield: 1 loaf

Breakfast Cookies

Full of healthy ingredients...good enough for breakfast!

3 cups rolled oats (preferably old-fashioned)
2 cups all-purpose flour
1 cup whole wheat flour
2 cups packed brown sugar
$^1/_2$ cup toasted wheat germ
2 teaspoons nutmeg, or 1 teaspoon nutmeg and
   1 teaspoon cinnamon
$1^1/_2$ teaspoons salt
$1^1/_2$ teaspoons baking soda
$^1/_2$ cup skim milk powder
1 cup (2 sticks) butter, at room temperature
$1^1/_2$ cups low-fat buttermilk, divided
2 cups (12 ounces) semisweet chocolate chips

1. Preheat the oven to 375 degrees. Lightly grease cookie sheets.
2. Mix the oats, flours, brown sugar, wheat germ, nutmeg, salt, baking soda and skim milk powder in a large bowl.
3. Cut the butter into small pieces and mix into the dry ingredients with a pastry blender.
4. Stir in $1^1/_4$ cups of the buttermilk and blend well.
5. Add the chocolate chips and stir to incorporate.
6. Drop golf ball size mounds 1 inch apart onto greased cookie sheets.
7. Lightly brush the top of the cookies with the remaining $^1/_4$ cup buttermilk.
8. Bake for about 15 to 17 minutes or until the edges are slightly browned.
9. Remove carefully (fragile while hot) to a wire rack to cool.
10. Will stay moist for up to 3 weeks if stored airtight.

♪ Can substitute raisins for the chocolate chips or add 1 cup raisins and 1 cup chopped walnuts.

 For sea level, cook for only 12 minutes.

Prep Time: 20 minutes   Cook Time: 15 to 17 minutes per batch   Yield: 5 dozen

Chinese Almond Cookies

A perfect end to an Asian meal.

2 cups all-purpose flour
$^1/_2$ cup white cornmeal
1 cup vegetable shortening
1 cup confectioners' sugar
2 eggs plus 1 egg yolk, divided
1 teaspoon almond extract
1 teaspoon water
Sesame seeds
Almonds (about 60), skins removed

1. Mix the flour and cornmeal in a medium bowl.
2. Cream the shortening, confectioners' sugar, 2 eggs and almond extract in a large bowl. Mix in the dry ingredients and chill for 1 hour.
3. Preheat the oven to 375 degrees.
4. Mix 1 egg yolk and water in a small bowl.
5. Shape the dough by rounded teaspoons. Dip into the egg mixture, then roll in sesame seeds. Place on an ungreased cookie sheet and top each with an almond.
6. Bake for 12 to 15 minutes.

Prep Time: 25 minutes   Chill Time: 1 hour

Cook Time: 12 to 15 minutes per batch   Yield: 5 dozen

Tuesday morning during the season, Festival Park is buzzing with the sounds of hundreds of happy children as they await the start of the entertaining and educational "Imagine That" youth concerts. The children eagerly hand over their tickets and find their seats. Suddenly, the tent is quiet as musicians, puppeteers, and dancers capture the attention of the young audience. Enrichment programs such as these reach far beyond the confines of the tent and the summer season. Throughout the year, Strings presents programs in schools and senior facilities, bringing the joy of music to all residents of the Yampa Valley.

Lemon Coconut Squares

A combination of the classic lemon squares and a delightful coconut top crust.

1/2 cup blanched whole almonds
1 1/2 cups all-purpose flour
1/2 cup confectioners' sugar
1 cup (2 sticks) very cold unsalted butter,
   cut into small pieces
1 cup sweetened flaked coconut
2 eggs
1 cup granulated sugar
1/2 teaspoon baking powder
1/4 teaspoon salt
1/3 cup lemon juice (from about 1 1/2 lemons)
1 1/2 teaspoons grated lemon zest

1. Preheat the oven to 350 degrees.
2. Grind the almonds in a food processor by pulsing until finely ground. Add the flour and confectioners' sugar; pulse to mix. Add the butter and blend with short pulses until the mixture resembles small crumbs.
3. Combine 2 cups of the almond mixture with the coconut in a small bowl. Set aside.
4. Press the remaining almond mixture onto the bottom of a 9x13-inch glass baking dish or metal pan, smoothing so that the top is even and gently pressed in.
5. Bake for about 17 minutes or until light golden brown.
6. Beat the eggs, granulated sugar, baking powder, salt and lemon juice in a bowl with an electric mixer until foamy. Stir in the lemon zest.
7. Pour the egg mixture over the baked crust. Sprinkle the reserved coconut mixture evenly on top.
8. Bake for 25 minutes, being careful not to let the coconut burn. Cover loosely with foil for the last 5 to 10 minutes if needed to prevent overbrowning.
9. Let cool thoroughly on a wire rack before cutting.

Prep Time: 20 minutes   Cook Time: 42 minutes   Yield: 24 bars

Lazy Daisy Cake

Easy and quick—a favorite for four generations.

2 eggs
1 cup less 2 tablespoons sugar
1 cup flour
3/4 teaspoon baking powder
1/4 teaspoon salt
1/2 cup hot milk
1 teaspoon vanilla extract
1 tablespoon butter, melted
5 tablespoons butter
9 tablespoons brown sugar
5 tablespoons cream or half-and-half
1 cup flaked coconut
1/2 cup chopped nuts

1. Preheat the oven to 350 degrees. Butter a 9x9-inch baking pan or spray with nonstick cooking spray.
2. Beat the eggs in a bowl. Add the sugar and beat well.
3. Mix the flour, baking powder and salt together. Add the flour mixture and milk alternately to the egg mixture.
4. Mix in the vanilla and melted butter. Pour into the prepared pan.
5. Bake for 25 minutes.
6. Combine 5 tablespoons butter, the brown sugar, cream, coconut and nuts in a saucepan and bring to a boil. Spread over the hot cake.
7. Place the cake under the broiler about 4 inches from the heat source for about 4 minutes or until the icing bubbles. Watch closely to prevent scorching.

♪ Peanut Butter Icing is a nice alternative. Combine 2 tablespoons peanut butter, 2 tablespoons softened butter, 2 cups confectioners' sugar, 3 tablespoons milk and 1/2 teaspoon vanilla extract. Beat together until fluffy and spread on the cooled cake.

For low altitude, use 1 cup sugar and 1 teaspoon baking powder.

Prep Time: 10 to 15 minutes   Cook Time: 25 minutes   Yield: 9 to12 servings

Key Lime Pie

On a Steamboat summer evening, nothing can be more
refreshing than this tart frozen pie.

1¼ cups graham cracker crumbs
5 tablespoons unsalted butter, melted
⅓ cup granulated sugar
3 egg yolks
Grated zest of 2 Key limes (about 1½ teaspoons)
1 can (14 ounces) sweetened condensed milk
⅔ cup fresh or bottled Key lime juice
1 cup heavy whipping cream, chilled
3 tablespoons confectioners' sugar

1. Preheat the oven to 350 degrees. Butter a 9-inch glass pie plate.
2. Place the graham cracker crumbs, butter and granulated sugar in a bowl and mix well.
3. Press the mixture onto the bottom and side of the pie plate, forming a neat border around the edge.
4. Bake for 8 minutes or until golden brown. Set aside to cool.
5. Beat the egg yolks and lime zest in a bowl with an electric mixer at high speed for about 5 minutes or until fluffy. Gradually add the condensed milk and beat for about 3 to 4 minutes or until thick. Reduce the mixer's speed and slowly add the lime juice, mixing just until combined.
6. Pour the mixture into the crust and bake for 10 minutes or until the filling is set.
7. Cool on a wire rack. Freeze for 15 to 20 minutes before serving.
8. Whip the whipping cream with the confectioners' sugar in a bowl until stiff peaks form.
9. Cut the pie into wedges and top with whipped cream.

Prep Time: 40 minutes   Cook Time: 18 minutes

Freeze Time: 15 to 20 minutes   Yield: 6 to 8 servings

Fresh Peach Pie

Fantastic with Colorado peaches.

Pastry for 1 (9-inch) pie
3 peaches, peeled and sliced (about 1 pound large peaches)
1 cup sugar
2 tablespoons cornstarch
1 cup sour cream

1. Preheat the oven to 450 degrees.
2. Roll out the pastry to an 11-inch circle. Place the pastry in a 9-inch pie plate, turning under the edges to fit. Crimp the edges.
3. Arrange the peaches on the pastry.
4. Mix the sugar and cornstarch. Combine with the sour cream in a bowl.
5. Pour the sour cream mixture over the peaches.
6. Bake for 10 minutes. Reduce oven temperature to 350 degrees. Bake for 50 to 60 minutes longer or until the top is light golden brown.

♪ To easily remove the skin from a peach, cover with boiling water and let stand for a minute or two. Remove and immerse in ice water to stop the cooking process. The skin should slide off easily.

Prep Time: 20 to 30 minutes　　Cook Time: 60 to 70 minutes
Yield: 6 to 8 servings

Western Colorado produces some of the best peaches in the country. The combination of high altitude, hot summer days, cool nights, and dry climate makes peach-growing risky but worth it, creating intensely flavored fruit with higher sugar and acids. They are luscious out of hand, or try some in this delicious pie.

Angel Food Bavarian Cream Cake

A prize-winning recipe.

Ever since 1876, when founding father James Crawford sponsored a picnic and flag-raising, Steamboat Springs residents have gathered together to celebrate the country's independence by recognizing the town's heritage. Community activities today include picnics, fireworks, and the main street parade, which just about everyone finds themselves marching in at some point in their lives. A rodeo has been part of the traditional festivities since 1903. Part of the Pro Rodeo series, cowboys and cowgirls compete in bareback and saddle bronc riding; calf, steer, and team roping; barrel racing; and bull riding. Children muster their courage for the ram and calf scrambles.

1 cup granulated sugar
2 tablespoons all-purpose flour
Pinch of salt
2 cups milk
4 egg yolks, beaten
1 package unflavored gelatin
$^1/_2$ cup hot water
$^1/_2$ pint (1 cup) heavy whipping cream, whipped
4 egg whites, stiffly beaten
1 angel food cake (homemade or store-bought)
$^1/_2$ pint (1 cup) heavy whipping cream, whipped with
   1 tablespoon confectioners' sugar and 1 tablespoon
   light corn syrup
Sliced fresh strawberries or raspberries for garnish

1. Mix the granulated sugar, flour and salt in a 2-quart nonstick saucepan. Blend in the milk and egg yolks. Cook over medium heat for about 8 minutes or until the mixture thickens to custard consistency, stirring constantly.
2. Mix the gelatin and hot water together. Set aside for 5 minutes and then add to the custard. Chill for at least 45 minutes in the refrigerator.
3. Fold the whipped cream into the custard. Fold in the beaten egg whites and chill for at least 2 hours.
4. Slice the angel food cake into 3 layers. Spread the Bavarian Cream over 1 cake layer. Top with a cake layer. Repeat the procedure with the remaining Bavarian Cream and cake layer. Top with the sweetened whipped cream. Refrigerate overnight.
5. Garnish with sliced strawberries or raspberries, if desired.

♪ Serve Bavarian Cream by itself in a large glass bowl or in individual wine glasses.

Prep Time: 40 minutes, divided   Cook Time: 8 to 10 minutes

Cool Time: 9 hours, divided   Yield: 1 cake

Galaktoboureko

You don't have to be able to pronounce it to fall in love with this amazing Greek dessert.

4 cups milk
2 cups heavy cream
1/2 cup plus 1 tablespoon
   farina (cream of wheat)
1 1/4 cups sugar, divided
6 egg yolks
1 tablespoon vanilla extract
1/2-3/4 cup butter

1/2-3/4 pound phyllo dough,
   thawed using the package
   directions
1/3 cup water
1 1/2 tablespoons fresh
   lemon juice
Cinnamon to sprinkle on top

1. Heat the milk and cream in a large saucepan until boiling.
2. Mix 1/2 cup sugar and the farina together and add to the milk mixture gradually. Return to a boil. Reduce the heat to medium-low and cook for about 5 to 10 minutes or until slightly thickened. Remove from the heat.
3. Beat the eggs and vanilla in a large bowl at high speed. Reduce the speed and gradually add the farina mixture to the eggs.
4. Melt the butter. Spread a thin layer over the bottom of a 9x13-inch pan using a pastry brush. Preheat the oven to 350 degrees.
5. Take the phyllo out of the packaging, and working as fast as you can, trim the phyllo sheets so that they are one inch larger than the pan on all four sides. Place one layer on the pan, spread melted butter on it, then another layer and repeat until you have seven layers, making sure the phyllo goes up the side of the pan.
6. Pour in the filling mixture and layer the remaining phyllo, approximately 8 to 10 more layers, as directed above, brushing each layer with butter. Do not go up the pan with these layers.
7. Score the top layer with a sharp knife into square serving-sized pieces, being careful not to score all the way through to the custard.
8. Bake for 35 to 45 minutes or until golden brown.
9. Combine 3/4 cup sugar and the water in a saucepan and bring to a boil. Boil for 8 minutes. Remove from the heat and stir in the lemon juice. Pour over the top and around the edge of the pan while hot. Let rest for 1 to 2 hours to allow the syrup to soak in.
10. Sprinkle with cinnamon before serving.

♪ Phyllo dough can be intimidating for some people, but it is really fun to use! Just work as quickly as you can, being careful as you separate each layer. Cover the phyllo with a damp cloth as you work to prevent it from drying out. You will have some leftover phyllo, which you can either throw out or use to make another small recipe that asks for phyllo. It will not keep very long after it is opened.

Prep time: 45 minutes   Cook time: 35 to 45 minutes   Yield: 15 servings

Meringue Cloud with Lemon Curd

*A combination of pavlova and angel pie, this beautiful
dessert deserves a standing ovation.*

MERINGUE
4 egg whites, at room
    temperature
Pinch of salt
1 cup plus 2 tablespoons
    sugar
2 teaspoons cornstarch
1 teaspoon white vinegar
A few drops of vanilla extract

LEMON CURD
3 ounces (6 tablespoons)
    unsalted butter, at room
    temperature

1 cup sugar
2 eggs
2 egg yolks
$2/3$ cup fresh lemon juice
    (about 3 lemons)
1 teaspoon grated lemon
    zest

CREAM
$1^{1}/_{2}$ cups heavy whipping
    cream
2 teaspoons light corn syrup

2 cups fresh raspberries

Preheat the oven to 350 degrees.

FOR THE MERINGUE:
1. Line a baking sheet with parchment paper. Trace a 10-inch circle on the paper.
2. Place the egg whites and salt in the bowl of a stand mixer fitted with the whisk
   attachment. Beat at medium-low speed for about 2 minutes or until frothy. Increase
   the speed to medium-high and beat for 2 to 3 minutes or until the egg whites form
   stiff but not dry peaks. Gradually add the sugar while whisking. Increase the speed
   to high and beat for 3 minutes or until stiff and glossy.
3. Sprinkle the cornstarch, vinegar and vanilla over the egg whites and gently fold in.
4. Fill the traced circle with meringue, smoothing the top and side to fill the circle. The
   meringue will spread as it bakes, so do not make it any larger than the circle.
5. Place on the center rack of the oven and reduce the oven temperature to 300 degrees.
   Bake for 1 hour. Turn off the oven and leave the meringue inside for about 4 hours
   or until completely cool.

FOR THE LEMON CURD:

1. Beat the butter and sugar in a large bowl with an electric mixer for about 2 minutes.
2. Slowly add the eggs and egg yolks and beat for 1 minute. Mix in the lemon juice. The mixture will look curdled but will smooth out as it cooks.
3. Pour the mixture into a medium-heavy saucepan and cook over low heat until the butter melts and the mixture looks smooth. Increase the heat to medium and cook for about 6 to 10 minutes or until the mixture thickens, stirring constantly. The mixture should leave a path on the back of a spoon and register 170 degrees on a candy thermometer. Do not boil.
4. Remove from the heat and stir in the lemon zest.
5. Pour into a bowl and place plastic wrap on the surface to keep a skin from forming. Chill in the refrigerator. The lemon curd will thicken as it cools.

FOR THE CREAM:

1. Place the chilled cream in a cold mixing bowl and whip to soft peaks. Add the corn syrup and whip for about 30 seconds longer.
2. To assemble, remove the baked meringue from the parchment and place on a cake plate. Mound whipped cream on top and spread to the edge. Spread lemon curd on top of the cream and carefully spread to cover. Mound raspberries on top of the lemon curd. Slice into wedges to serve.

Prep Time: 50 minutes   Cook Time: 1 hour   Cool Time: 4 hours

Yield: 12 servings, 2 inch wedges

Autumn

Autumn's leaf display of red gambel oak, yellow aspen, and rich evergreen provides a shifting medley of colors.

PHOTOGRAPH BY CHRIS SELBY

Early Hunter's Feast

Giovanni's Portobello
68

Orange Almond Salad
75

Grilled Quail with Jalapeño Plum Sauce
85

Wild Rice Pilaf
96

Bavarian Apple Torte
107

Family Night

Southwest Pumpkin Bisque
72

Corn, Avocado, & Tomato Salad
76

Turkey Rellenos Casserole
83

Double-Chocolate Brownies
100

Turning cottonwood trees invite contemplations along the Yampa River.

Asiago Cheese Dip

Rich and warm, this party appetizer can be assembled ahead of time.

1/2 cup sliced green onions
1/4 cup thinly sliced
  mushrooms
1/4 cup sun-dried tomatoes,
  finely chopped
1 cup mayonnaise or light
  mayonnaise

1 cup (8 ounces) sour cream
  or low-fat sour cream
1/2 cup (2 ounces) grated
  asiago cheese, divided
French bread or crackers

1. Preheat the oven to 350 degrees.
2. Combine the green onions, mushrooms, sun-dried tomatoes, mayonnaise, sour cream and all but 2 tablespoons of the cheese in a bowl. Spoon into a 1-quart baking dish. Sprinkle the remaining cheese over the top. Bake for 30 minutes.
3. Serve with French bread rounds or crackers.

Prep Time: 15 minutes   Cook Time: 30 minutes   Yield: 2 1/2 to 3 cups

Spinach Artichoke Dip

A popular appetizer from Blue Bonnet Catering.

CHEF MELISSA CARTAN

1 bunch fresh spinach,
  washed
1 cup artichoke hearts
1/4 red onion
1 tablespoon chopped garlic
1 cup shredded Parmesan
  cheese, plus additional for
  baguette top

2 tablespoons lemon juice
1/2 cup mayonnaise
Salt and freshly ground
  pepper to taste
1 baguette
Olive oil
Italian seasoning

1. Sauté the spinach in a skillet for a few minutes or until wilted. Place the spinach, artichoke hearts, onion and garlic in a food processor and pulse 10 to12 times. Pour into a bowl. Mix in 1 cup of the cheese, the lemon juice, mayonnaise, salt and pepper.
2. Preheat the oven to 375 degrees.
3. Slice the baguette and place on a baking sheet. Drizzle the slices with olive oil and sprinkle with Italian seasoning and the remaining cheese. Bake for 8 to10 minutes or until golden brown.
4. Microwave the dip on High for about 2 minutes. Serve with baguette slices.

Prep Time: 20 minutes   Cook Time: 12 minutes   Yield: 10 to 12 servings

Autumn is a relatively short season famous for its stunning blue skies. The locals savor each and every warm day like bites of a favorite comfort food. While some people are counting the days until the snow flies, others are basking in the delightful Indian summers Colorado often bestows upon us.

Cilantro Mousse

Even cilantro skeptics will change their tune once they taste this light and refreshing starter.

1 bunch cilantro, bottom stems removed
1 package (8 ounces) cream cheese, softened
1/2 cup mayonnaise
1 clove garlic, peeled
1/2 cup chopped onion
2 serrano chiles, stemmed, seeded and chopped
1/4 cup hot water
1 envelope unflavored gelatin
1/4 cup cold water
1 teaspoon salt
1/2 teaspoon freshly ground pepper
Pita chips

1. Combine the cilantro, cream cheese, mayonnaise, garlic, onion and chiles in a food processor and purée until smooth.
2. Combine the hot water and gelatin in a small bowl, stirring until dissolved. Add the cold water and stir.
3. Add the gelatin mixture, salt and pepper to the cilantro mixture in the food processor and blend. Add more salt and pepper if necessary.
4. Pour into an oiled mold and refrigerate for several hours or until firm.
5. Serve with pita chips

Prep Time: 10 minutes   Chill Time: 2 hours   Yield: 10 servings

Horseradish Shrimp

2 1/2 teaspoons bottled
  horseradish
1 package (8 ounces) cream
  cheese, low fat or regular
3 tablespoons mayonnaise
1 clove garlic, minced
1 tablespoon chopped fresh
  parsley

2 tablespoons chopped onion
1 tablespoon chopped
  fresh dill
1 cup cooked shrimp,
  chopped (about 8 ounces)
Salt and pepper to taste
Parsley and lemon slices
  for garnish

1. Process the horseradish, cream cheese, mayonnaise and garlic in a food processor until smooth. Spoon into a small bowl. Stir in the parsley, onion, dill and shrimp. Season with salt and pepper.
2. Spoon into a glass or ceramic dish. Refrigerate for 1 hour.
3. Garnish with parsley and lemon slices. Serve with crackers or cucumber rounds.

Prep Time: 20 minutes   Chill Time: 1 hour   Yield: 2 cups

Stuffed Mushrooms with Spinach and Cheese

A delicious low calorie appetizer that can be quickly cooked in the microwave.

1 package (10 ounces) frozen
  spinach, thawed and water
  squeezed out
1/2 cup finely chopped
  green onions
1/2 cup finely chopped parsley
4 ounces feta cheese,
  crumbled

1/2 cup grated
  Parmesan cheese
Salt and pepper to taste
24 mushrooms (about
  1 pound), cleaned and
  stems removed

1. Combine the spinach, green onions, parsley, feta cheese, Parmesan cheese, salt and pepper in a bowl and mix well. Chill, covered, until ready to stuff the mushrooms.
2. Spoon the mixture into the mushroom caps. Arrange the stuffed mushrooms on a microwavable serving dish.
3. Microwave for 2 to 4 minutes or until the filling is hot and bubbly. Microwave ovens vary, so check the mushrooms after 2 minutes. Serve hot.

Prep Time: 15 minutes   Cook Time: 2 to 4 minutes   Yield: 24 servings

Grill portobello mushrooms instead of beef, as they are very hearty and have an earthy, woodsy taste. Brush with a little olive oil and place on the grill with the gill side up in order to retain their juices, for about 8 to 10 minutes. Cremini are small portobello mushrooms and have a similar flavor.

Giovanni's Portobello

Giovanni's is located downtown in the historic Soda Creek building.
They serve Northern Italian cuisine in an intimate setting.

2 large portobello mushroom caps,
   washed and stems removed
$^1/_4$ cup olive oil
1 tablespoon chopped garlic
$^1/_2$ to $^2/_3$ cup crumbled goat cheese
2 tablespoons roasted red bell peppers
   (2-ounce glass jar in grocery store), chopped
1 tablespoon pine nuts, toasted
2 teaspoons chopped fresh basil

1. Preheat the oven to 350 degrees.
2. Coat the mushrooms with the olive oil. Top with the garlic. Place on a baking sheet. Bake for 30 minutes.
3. Top with the goat cheese and roasted red peppers. Bake for 3 minutes longer.
4. Top with the pine nuts and basil.
5. Slice into squares or wedges. Serve on a plate.

Prep Time: 15 minutes   Cook time: 33 minutes   Yield: 4 to 6 servings

Spinach Quesadilla Wedges

*Great snacks anytime, these baked quesadillas can be made
ahead using any of your favorite ingredients.*

8 fajita-size flour tortillas
3 cups (12 ounces) shredded pepper Jack cheese
1 cup chopped red onion
2 cups shredded spinach leaves

1. Preheat the oven to 425 degrees.
2. Place 4 tortillas on a baking sheet. Layer half the cheese, all the onion, all the spinach, the remaining 4 tortillas and the remaining cheese over the tortillas on the baking sheet.
3. Bake for 8 to 10 minutes.
4. Let cool for 5 minutes before cutting each tortilla into eight wedges.
5. Can be refrigerated and then reheated at 350 degrees for 10 minutes.

Serving Suggestion: Guacamole and sour cream are good accompaniments.

 Some variations are Cheddar cheese and 1 can (4 ounces) diced green chiles or chopped cooked shrimp, plain Monterey Jack cheese, and 1 can (4 ounces) diced green chiles.

Prep Time: 30 minute   Cook Time: 8 to 10 minutes
Yield: 12 servings, 32 wedges

Pot Stickers

The Cottonwood Grill serves creative Pacific Rim cuisine. Their location overlooks the Yampa River. Check out their Lamb Pot Stickers, Ponzu Sauce, and Sweet Chinese Mustard Sauce.

CHEFS PETER LAUTNER & MICHAEL FRAGOLA

POT STICKERS
Lamb, pork, turkey or
   mushroom filling
   (see recipes on page 71)
Round won ton wrappers

2 egg yolks, beaten
Vegetable oil or sesame oil
Ponzu Sauce or Sweet
   Chinese Mustard Sauce
   (see recipes below)

1. Scoop 1 to 1 1/2 tablespoons of the filling of your choice into the center of each won ton wrapper. Brush the edges with egg yolk or water and seal together. Be sure the won ton wrapper dries completely sealed.
2. Brush a bamboo basket with oil and lay the pot stickers in the basket.
3. Steam until firm to the touch
   a. For lamb variation, 7 to 9 minutes
   b. For pork variation, 10 to 12 minutes
   c. For turkey variation, 15 minutes
   d. For mushroom variation, 10 minutes
4. Serve the meat variations with the sauce of your choice. Serve the mushroom variation with melted butter and freshly ground black pepper.

PONZU SAUCE
1/4 cup rice vinegar
1/4 cup sugar
1/8 cup mirin
1 cup light soy sauce

1/2 cup water
1 tablespoon green onions,
   sliced diagonally
1 tablespoon minced ginger

Combine the rice vinegar, sugar, mirin, soy sauce and water in a bowl and mix until blended. Add the green onions and ginger and mix well.

Prep Time: 10 minutes   Yield: 2 cups

SWEET CHINESE
   MUSTARD SAUCE
2 teaspoons rice wine
   vinegar

2 tablespoons honey
1/4 cup dry mustard
1/4 cup mayonnaise
6 tablespoons water

Combine the rice wine vinegar, honey, mustard, mayonnaise and water in a bowl and mix well. Allow the flavors to combine for 6 hours.

Prep Time: 5 minutes   Stand Time: 6 hours   Yield: 1 cup

Variations on a Theme

LAMB FILLING

2½ pounds ground lamb
6 tablespoons minced peeled fresh ginger
2 tablespoons minced garlic
1 red Thai chile, fresh, seeded, minced
2 teaspoons salt
2 teaspoons pepper

Combine the lamb, ginger, garlic, red chile, salt and pepper in a skillet and sauté briefly. Adjust the seasonings to taste.

PORK FILLING

1 pound ground pork
4 ounces spicy Italian sausage
¼ cup minced peeled fresh ginger
3 garlic cloves, minced
2 tablespoons ground fresh chili paste
Salt to taste
Fresh ground pepper to taste

Combine the pork, Italian sausage, ginger, garlic, chili paste, salt and pepper in a bowl and mix well.

TURKEY FILLING

1 pound ground turkey
1 teaspoon minced peeled fresh ginger
2 garlic cloves, minced
¼ teaspoon Thai chile paste
¼ cup minced red bell pepper
¼ cup minced celery
¼ cup low-sodium soy sauce
2 tablespoons minced green onions
1 tablespoon dry sherry
1 tablespoon cornstarch
½ teaspoon dark sesame oil

Combine the turkey, ginger, garlic, chile paste, bell pepper, celery, soy sauce, green onions, sherry, cornstarch and sesame oil in a bowl and mix well.

MUSHROOM FILLING

½ medium onion, minced
1 tablespoon olive oil
12 ounces fresh mushrooms, chopped, or 1 ounce dried porcini mushrooms, reconstituted and chopped
Salt to taste

1. Sauté the onion in the olive oil in a sauté pan for 8 to 10 minutes or until translucent and pale golden brown. Add the mushrooms and cook for 2 to 3 minutes, stirring constantly. Season with salt.
2. Remove from the heat and let stand until cool.

Prep Time: 25 minutes   Wrap Time: 30 minutes

Cook Time: 7 to 20 minutes   Yield: 35 to 64 pot stickers

Southwest Pumpkin Bisque

This soup is smoky and slightly sweet, with the wonderful flavor of pumpkin.

2 ears of corn, shucked
1 (2^1/$_2$ pound) pumpkin
1 tablespoon olive oil
1 onion, chopped
1 carrot, chopped
1 garlic clove, minced
1 bottle (12 ounces)
   pumpkin ale or
   Oktoberfest beer
1^1/$_2$ cups vegetable stock
^{1}/$_2$ cup half-and-half
^{1}/$_4$ teaspoon chile pepper,
   ground
^{1}/$_4$ teaspoon sweet paprika

^{1}/$_4$ teaspoon sage, rubbed
^{1}/$_4$ teaspoon allspice
^{1}/$_4$ teaspoon nutmeg
^{1}/$_4$ teaspoon ginger
3 tablespoons pure maple
   syrup
Salt and cayenne pepper
   to taste
^{1}/$_2$ to 1 pound aged
   Emmentaler cheese,
   shredded
1 red bell pepper, finely
   chopped
Sprinkle of paprika

1. Roast the corn on the grill, rotating every few minutes. Set aside to cool. Cut the kernels off the corn cobs. This can be done a day ahead.
2. Preheat the oven to 350 degrees. Spray a foil-lined sheet baking pan with oil.
3. Cut the pumpkin into halves and scoop out the seeds. Place cut side down in the pan. Bake for 30 minutes. Let stand until cool to the touch. Peel off the skin. Can be prepared a day ahead.
4. Heat the olive oil in a heavy-bottomed stockpot. Sauté the onion, carrot, garlic and corn in the hot oil. Add the pumpkin ale and cook for 20 minutes or until reduced by ^{1}/$_2$ or more.
5. Place the mixture in a food processor and purée until almost smooth. Add the pumpkin and purée again until smooth.
6. Combine the puréed mixture, vegetable stock and half-and-half in the stockpot. Bring to a low simmer.
7. Mix in the chile pepper, paprika, sage, allspice, nutmeg, ginger, maple syrup, salt and cayenne pepper.
8. Ladle the hot soup into bowls and top each with cheese. Sprinkle with bell pepper and paprika.

♪ You may substitute 2^1/$_2$ cups canned pumpkin for fresh pumpkin if desired.

Prep Time: 15 minutes   Cook Time: 1 hour 45 minutes   Yield: 6 servings

French Market Soup

The intense flavor is your reward for slowly simmering beans and vegetables. Package the extra beans and give to friends along with this delicious recipe.

¹/4 cup navy beans
¹/4 cup red beans
¹/4 cup lentils
¹/4 cup black beans
¹/4 cup garbanzo beans
¹/4 cup barley
¹/4 cup pinto beans
¹/4 cup split peas
¹/4 cup baby lima beans
¹/4 cup black-eyed peas
3 quarts water
Ham hocks or ham bone
1 bay leaf
1 teaspoon thyme
Dash of red pepper
  (flakes or powder)

1 quart tomatoes, diced
  (32 ounces)
6 ribs celery, chopped
1 large green bell pepper,
  chopped
2 garlic cloves, minced
2 tablespoons salt
1 whole chicken, cut into
  pieces
1 pound smoked sausage
  (can be turkey sausage),
  cut into 1-inch pieces
2 to 3 tablespoons chopped
  parsley
Salt

1. Rinse all the beans and peas and place in a large bowl. Cover with water. Soak overnight.
2. Drain the beans and peas and place in a large kettle (an 8-quart stockpot will work if that's all you have, but larger is better). Add the water, ham hocks, bay leaf, thyme and red pepper. Cover and simmer for 2¹/2 to 3 hours or until the beans are tender.
3. Add the tomatoes, celery, bell pepper and garlic. Simmer for 1¹/2 hours.
4. Add the chicken, sausage, parsley and salt. Simmer for about 1 hour or until chicken is cooked through.
5. Remove the chicken and let cool. Remove and discard the skin and bones. Cut the chicken into small pieces and return to the soup.
6. Remove the ham hocks, cut the ham from the hocks and return to the soup.
7. Reheat, adding more water if the soup is too thick. Serve hot.

Prep Time: 1 hour   Soak Time: Overnight   Cook Time: 5¹/2 hours
Yield: 14 to 16 servings

Cape May Clam Chowder

Enjoy this New England-style chowder.

6 ounces bacon
3 onions, finely chopped
8 ounces mushrooms, finely chopped
3 garlic cloves, minced
1 tablespoon flour
2 bottles (8 ounces each) clam juice
4 cups milk
3 tablespoons butter
6 potatoes, peeled and cut into $\frac{1}{2}$-inch cubes
Salt and pepper to taste
2 cans (10 ounces each) whole baby clams,
    including juice
3 cans ($6\frac{1}{2}$ ounces each) chopped clams,
    including juice
1 cup light cream
1 large pinch of saffron
3 tablespoons chopped fresh parsley

1. Cook the bacon slowly in a large Dutch oven for about 10 minutes or until the fat is rendered. Increase the heat and brown the bacon. Drain on paper towels and crumble.
2. Stir the onions, mushrooms and garlic into the bacon drippings and cook slowly to soften. Do not brown.
3. Stir in the flour, clam juice, milk, butter, potatoes, salt and pepper. Cover and bring to a boil. Reduce the heat to medium-low and cook for 10 minutes or until the potatoes begin to soften. If you like a thicker soup, purée $\frac{1}{2}$ of the potato mixture in a food processor and then return to the Dutch oven.
4. Add the whole and chopped clams, cream, saffron and bacon. Simmer for 7 to 10 minutes or until the potatoes are tender.
5. Add the chopped parsley and serve.

Prep Time: 30 minutes   Cook Time: 35 to 40 minutes   Yield: 8 to 10 servings

Orange Almond Salad

The caramelized almonds make this spinach salad unique.

4 tablespoons sugar, divided
1/2 cup almonds
1/2 teaspoon salt
1/2 teaspoon freshly ground pepper
1/4 cup salad oil
2 tablespoons balsamic vinegar
6 ounces (or more) baby spinach, stems removed
1 tablespoon minced fresh parsley
2 green onions with tops, sliced
1 can (11 ounces) mandarin oranges, drained

1. For the caramelized almonds, heat 2 tablespoons of the sugar and the almonds in a heavy skillet over low heat until the sugar turns brown and sticks to the almonds, stirring constantly. Place on waxed paper and let cool. Break the almonds apart.
2. Prepare the dressing. Combine the salt, pepper, remaining 2 tablespoons sugar, salad oil and balsamic vinegar in a jar with a tight-fitting lid and shake well.
3. Mix the spinach, parsley and green onions in a salad bowl.
4. Toss the spinach mixture with the dressing.
5. Arrange the caramelized almonds and oranges on top.

Prep Time: 20 minutes   Yield: 4 to 6 servings

The Kitchen Tour began as a fundraiser for Steamboat Seasons. The event offers the opportunity to visit kitchens in private homes to view the latest in kitchen design, décor, and equipment. Local chefs demonstrate their culinary skills and share their cooking secrets, many of which are included in this book.

Corn, Avocado, & Tomato Salad

This versatile combination of vegetables makes a crowd pleasing side salad.

1 to 2 pints cherry tomatoes, halved
1 can (11 ounces) corn, drained, or use frozen corn,
  about 1 1/2 cups
1/4 cup finely chopped red onion
1 can (15 ounces) black beans, drained (optional)
Red Wine Vinaigrette (see recipe below)
3 or 4 large ripe avocados, peeled and cubed
  (prepare just before serving)

1. Mix the tomatoes, corn, onions and beans in a serving bowl.
2. Pour the vinaigrette over the vegetable mixture.
3. Just before serving, gently stir in the avocados.

Serving Suggestion: Grilled fish or chicken are great accompaniments.

Prep Time: 20 minute   Yield: 8 to 10 servings

Red Wine Vinaigrette

1 tablespoon red wine vinegar
1/4 cup good-quality olive oil
Salt and pepper to taste

1. Combine the vinegar, olive oil, salt and pepper in a bowl and whisk until blended.
2. Use immediately or store in a jar with a tight-fitting lid in the refrigerator.

Creamy Coleslaw

1/2 onion, chopped
1/2 cup sugar
1/2 cup vegetable oil
1/4 cup cider vinegar
3 tablespoons mayonnaise
1/4 teaspoon celery seeds

1/2 teaspoon salt
1/4 teaspoon freshly
   ground pepper
1 cabbage, shredded, or
   1 1/2 pounds prepackaged
   shredded cabbage

1. Combine the onion and sugar in a bowl. Cover and let stand for 30 minutes.
2. Pour the onion mixture into a blender. Add the oil, vinegar, mayonnaise, celery seeds, salt and pepper. Blend well.
3. Cover and refrigerate for at least 1 hour.
4. Just before serving, toss the dressing with the cabbage.

Prep Time: 15 minutes   Stand Time: 30 minutes   Chill Time: 1 hour

Yield: 1 1/2 cups dressing

Tugboat Pasta Salad

The Tugboat Grill & Pub is ranked among the top 10 ski bars in America.
It is located in Ski Time Square.

CHEF KENYON COXON

1 1/4 pounds tri-color
   pasta spirals
1/2 cup puréed seeded
   cherry peppers
1/2 cup puréed seeded
   pepperoncini
1 green bell pepper, diced
3/4 red bell pepper, diced
1/2 red onion, diced
1/2 cup (2 ounces) grated
   Parmesan cheese

3/4 cup olive oil
2 tablespoons
   red wine vinegar
2 tablespoons
   balsamic vinegar
1 tablespoon fresh
   basil leaves, torn
   into small pieces
Salt and freshly ground
   pepper to taste

1. Fill a large stockpot 1/2 full with water and bring to a boil. Add the pasta and cook until al dente using the package directions. Drain and cool; set aside.
2. Combine the pasta, bell peppers, onion, cheese, olive oil, vinegars, basil, salt and pepper. in a bowl and mix well.
3. Keep refrigerated and serve chilled. It's best the next day.

Prep Time: 30 minutes   Yield: 12 to 15 servings

Meat Loaf with Zesty Tomato Sauce

The sauce makes this meat loaf special. Real comfort food on a cold Steamboat night.

MEAT LOAF
1 pound ground beef or ground buffalo
1/4 cup chopped onion
1/4 cup dry bread crumbs
1 egg
Salt and pepper to taste

SAUCE
1 can (8 ounces) tomato sauce
1 can water (to rinse out can)
2 tablespoons apple cider vinegar
1 to 2 tablespoons brown sugar
1 teaspoon mustard
A few drops of lemon juice
1 small onion, chopped (about 1/2 cup)
1/2 teaspoon horseradish
1/2 teaspoon Worcestershire sauce

FOR THE MEAT LOAF:
1. Preheat the oven to 350 degrees.
2. Mix the ground beef, onion, bread crumbs, egg, salt and pepper in a bowl and shape into a loaf. Place in a 7x11-inch baking dish and set aside.

FOR THE SAUCE:
1. Mix all ingredients in a bowl and pour over the meat loaf. It will seem like too much sauce, but as it bakes the sauce reduces and thickens.
2. Bake for 1 hour and 15 minutes, basting meat loaf 2 or 3 times.

This sauce is also good with baked pork chops: Season 4 to 6 chops with salt and pepper and place in large baking pan. Pour sauce over the chops and cover with foil. Bake at 350 degrees for 1 1/2 to 2 hours.

Prep Time: 15 minutes   Cook Time: 1 hour 15 minutes   Yield: 4 servings

Apricot Roast Pork

The sweet-tart flavor of this sauce makes it a great fall dish, and the ease of preparation makes it perfect for entertaining.

1 boneless pork loin (5 to 6 pounds),
   tied with kitchen string
Salt and freshly ground pepper to taste
6 tablespoons butter, divided
1 cup light red wine, such as pinot noir
Bouquet garni (1 bay leaf, 6 to 8 fresh thyme sprigs
   and 2 fresh sage leaves, tied together with kitchen string)
$1/4$ cup port
$1/4$ cup veal demi-glace (available at specialty food stores)
1 cup chicken broth
$1/4$ cup apricot jam
$1/4$ cup slivered dried apricots, soaked in water
   for 20 to 30 minutes
Pomegranate seeds for garnish

1. Preheat the oven to 350 degrees. Season the pork with salt and pepper.
2. Melt 3 tablespoons of the butter in a large roasting pan over medium-high heat. Add the pork and cook for 4 to 5 minutes per side or until brown.
3. Add the wine and bouquet garni. Cover and bake for $1^1/2$ to 2 hours, basting occasionally. The pork should register about 145 degrees on an instant-read thermometer for medium. Remove the pork to a warm platter and cover. Discard the bouquet garni.
4. Place the roasting pan over medium-high heat and add the port to deglaze, scraping up any browned bits.
5. Combine the demi-glace and chicken broth in a bowl and add to the pan. Stir in the apricot jam and drained apricots. Cook over high heat for 8 to 10 minutes or until the sauce is thick enough to coat a spoon. Enrich the sauce with the remaining 3 tablespoons butter. Season to taste with salt and pepper.
6. Cut the pork into $1/2$-inch-thick slices. Garnish with pomegranate seeds. Serve the sauce on the side.

Serving Suggestion: Serve with long grain and wild rice mix or mashed potatoes and steamed sweet peas.

As a substitute for the demi-glace, reduce 1 can (14 ounces) beef broth to $1/4$ cup by boiling vigorously in an uncovered saucepan.

Prep Time: 10 minutes   Cook Time: 1 hour 45 minutes   Yield: 8 servings

Pork Marsala

On a chilly fall evening, this warming and elegant dish is quick to prepare.

1 (1-pound) pork tenderloin, trimmed
Salt and freshly ground pepper
1 tablespoon butter
1 tablespoon olive oil
1 garlic clove, minced
1 tablespoon tomato paste
1/2 cup dry marsala
1/2 cup dry red wine
8 ounces fresh mushroom caps, quartered if large
1 tablespoon chopped fresh parsley

1. Season the pork with salt and pepper.
2. Heat the butter and olive oil in a large heavy skillet over medium-high heat until hot but not smoking. Brown the tenderloin on all sides. Remove from the skillet and keep warm in a 200-degree oven.
3. Reduce the heat to medium. Add the garlic to the skillet and sauté for about 1 minute or until it begins to brown. Mix the tomato paste with the wines and add to the skillet with the mushrooms. Stir to blend with the pan juices, scraping up any browned bits. Simmer for 3 to 5 minutes.
4. Return the tenderloin to the skillet. Cover and simmer to medium-rare, about 145 degrees with an instant-read thermometer. Remove the tenderloin to a warmed platter and let stand for 5 to 10 minutes.
5. Boil the sauce until reduced a bit.
6. Cut the tenderloin diagonally into 1/2-inch slices. Serve with the sauce. Garnish with fresh parsley.

Serving Suggestion: Serve with mashed potatoes and a green vegetable of your choice.

Prep Time: 20 minutes   Cook Time: 30 minutes   Yield: 3 to 4 servings

Roasted Pork Tenderloin with Sage Crust

The crunchy crust on this pork tenderloin is irresistible.

1 (1-pound) pork tenderloin, trimmed
Salt and freshly ground pepper
1 tablespoon olive oil
1 tablespoon butter
2 garlic cloves, minced
2 corn muffins, crumbled
1 teaspoon finely chopped fresh sage
2 tablespoons Dijon mustard

1. Preheat the oven to 425 degrees. Oil a shallow roasting pan. Season the pork with salt and pepper.
2. Heat the olive oil in a large skillet and brown the pork on all sides. Remove to the roasting pan.
3. Add the butter and garlic to the skillet and sauté for about 1 minute or until browned. Turn off the heat and stir in the muffin crumbs and sage.
4. Brush the mustard over the pork and pat the crumbs over the surface.
5. Roast in the oven to 145 degrees, about 15 to 20 minutes. (Check after 15 minutes to see if the crumbs are getting too dark. If they are, tent loosely with foil.) Remove from the oven. Cover with foil and let stand for 10 minutes.
6. Cut into ¹/₂-inch-thick slices.

Serving Suggestion: This recipe is good served with mashed or roasted potatoes and a green vegetable.

Sea level may need less cooking time.

Prep Time: 20 minutes   Cook Time: 20 minutes   Yield: 3 to 4 servings

Grown primarily in small family orchards on the Western slope, many of them organic, Colorado pears benefit from our intense sunlight, cool nights, and pure alpine water. One of the few fruits that must be picked unripe, pears ripen on their own at room temperature. To hasten the process place them in a brown paper bag. Excellent on salads, as part of entrees and desserts, or as a healthy snack.

Chicken Breasts with Pears

Use Bosc or Anjou pears in this nice fall dish.

4 boneless skinless chicken breasts
Salt and freshly ground pepper
1 tablespoon olive oil
1 tablespoon butter
2 fresh pears, peeled, cored and sliced into
    8 wedges each
2 tablespoons orange juice
2 tablespoons brown sugar
1/4 teaspoon cinnamon
1/4 cup sherry

1. Season the chicken with salt and pepper.
2. Heat the olive oil in a 12-inch sauté pan over medium heat. Add the chicken and sauté for about 8 to 10 minutes or until brown and no longer pink in the center, turning once. Remove to a warmed plate.
3. Melt the butter in the sauté pan and add the pears. Cook for about 2 minutes, stirring frequently.
4. Combine the orange juice, brown sugar, cinnamon and sherry in a bowl. Pour over the pears and cook for 1 minute to thicken the syrup.
5. Return the chicken and any juices to the pan and simmer gently for 1 to 2 minutes to heat through.

Serving Suggestion: Serve with rice or Carrot & Sweet Potato Purée (see recipe on page 92).

Prep Time: 10 minutes   Cook Time: 15 minutes   Yield: 4 servings

Turkey Rellenos Casserole

A very good and different Mexican dish and a great way to use leftover turkey.

1 can (10 ounces) mild enchilada sauce
8 (6-inch) corn tortillas
1 tablespoon butter
1 cup chopped onion
3 eggs
1 cup milk
1 can (17 ounces) creamed corn
2 to 3 cups (8 to 12 ounces) shredded Cheddar cheese
1 cup shredded jalapeno Jack cheese
2 tablespoons chopped parsley
1 tablespoon lemon juice
2 to 3 cups shredded cooked turkey, divided
2 cans (7 ounces each) whole green chiles, drained,
   split lengthwise

1. Preheat the oven to 325 degrees. Grease a 9x13-inch baking dish.
2. Pour the enchilada sauce into a shallow bowl. Dip 4 of the tortillas in the enchilada sauce and place in the baking dish. Set aside.
3. Melt the butter in a 10-inch skillet over medium heat. Add the onion and sauté lightly.
4. Beat the eggs in a large bowl. Add the milk, sautéed onion, corn, cheeses, parsley and lemon juice and stir to combine.
5. Pour half the egg mixture over the tortillas in the baking dish. Sprinkle with half the turkey. Dip the remaining 4 tortillas in the enchilada sauce and layer on top of the turkey. Top with the remaining egg mixture.
6. Sprinkle with the remaining turkey and arrange the chiles on top.
7. Bake for 1 hour and 15 minutes or until the top is brown.

Serving Suggestion: Serve with black beans and green salad or guacamole.

 You may vary the spiciness by using plain Monterey Jack cheese and reducing the amount of green chiles used.

Prep Time: 35 minutes   Cook Time: 1 hour 15 minutes   Yield: 8 to 10 servings

Duck Breast with Cranberry Orange Sauce

2 duck breasts (8 ounces)
1/2 tablespoon soy sauce
1/2 teaspoon pepper
1/2 teaspoon granulated garlic
1/2 tablespoon grated orange zest
Cranberry Orange Sauce (see recipe below)

1. Score the skin on the duck breast in a crisscross pattern (do not cut the meat).
2. Mix the soy sauce, pepper, garlic and orange zest in a shallow dish. Add the duck and marinate in the refrigerator for 1 hour, turning every 15 minutes.
3. Preheat the oven to 350 degrees. Remove the duck from the marinade and discard the marinade.
4. Roast the duck skin side up for about 30 to 40 minutes or until it reaches 165 degrees and the fat is mostly rendered.
5. Serve with Cranberry Orange Sauce.

Prep Time: 15 minutes   Marinate Time: 1 hour   Cook Time: 30 to 40 minutes

Yield: 2 servings

Cranberry Orange Sauce

1 cup orange juice
1 cup apple juice
3 ounces dried cranberries, chopped
   (may substitute craisins)
1 tablespoon grated orange zest
2 tablespoons cornstarch
2 tablespoons water
1 teaspoon orange liqueur
1/2 cup (1 stick) butter, chopped
Salt to taste
Brown sugar to taste

1. Simmer the juices in a saucepan. Add the cranberries and orange zest. Simmer until the cranberries have softened.
2. Combine the cornstarch and water in a bowl and mix well. Stir into the sauce until thickened. Add the orange liqueur.
3. Remove from the heat. Whisk in the butter until it fully emulsifies.
4. Adjust flavor with salt and brown sugar.

Grilled Quail with Jalapeño Plum Sauce

The unusual blend of fruit, peppers, curry, and soy will keep your guests talking about this sauce. The perfect glaze for any white meat and a most delightful dipping sauce for spring rolls.

Cornish game hen can be substituted for quail.

CHEF DAVID NELSON

JALAPEÑO PLUM SAUCE
2¹/₂ tablespoons soybean oil
¹/₃ cup finely diced red onion
1¹/₂ tablespoons minced
  garlic
1¹/₂ jalapeño chiles, seeds
  and ribs removed,
  chopped
1¹/₂ pounds purple plums,
  pitted and finely diced
¹/₂ tablespoon curry powder

¹/₂ teaspoon allspice
¹/₂ cup honey
¹/₄ cup soy sauce
Juice of 1 orange and
  2 lemons

QUAIL
8 semi-boneless quail
Vegetable oil
Salt to taste

FOR THE SAUCE:
1. Heat the soybean oil in a large heavy stockpot. Sauté the onion, garlic, and jalapeño chiles in the hot oil for 10 minutes or until tender. Stir in the plums, curry powder and allspice.
2. Once the spices are dispersed, mix in the honey, soy sauce and juices. Cook over medium-low heat for 1 hour and 15 minutes, stirring frequently. The consistency should be like chunky tomato sauce.
3. Remove from the heat and let cool to room temperature. Bottle and chill the sauce.

FOR THE QUAIL:
1. Preheat the grill to medium.
2. Brush both sides of the quail lightly with oil and season with salt. Place breast side down on the grill. Grill until the skin starts to bubble and brown a little. Turn breast side up and baste liberally with Jalapeño Plum Sauce. Don't be afraid of the sauce being too spicy, as most of the heat from the jalapeño comes from the discarded seeds and ribs. Continue to turn and baste the quail every couple of minutes or so until the quail are firm and have a nice glaze, about 10 minutes depending on your grill. Serve hot off the grill with a ramekin of sauce on the side.

Prep Time: 30 minutes   Cook Time: 1 hour 15 minutes   Yield: 4 servings

Basil Shrimp with Feta & Orzo

Very tasty and no cleanup!

To store basil at season's end, pick the leaves from the plant, wash, and pat dry. Finely chop and mix with enough olive oil to make a paste. Spoon tablespoonfuls into ice cube trays and freeze. Remove and place in freezer bags.

1/2 cup uncooked orzo
2 teaspoons olive oil, divided
1 cup diced tomatoes
3/4 cup sliced green onions
1/2 cup crumbled feta or blue cheese
1/2 teaspoon grated lemon zest
1 tablespoon fresh lemon juice
1/4 teaspoon salt
1/4 teaspoon pepper
12 ounces large shrimp, peeled and deveined
1/4 cup chopped fresh basil

1. Preheat the oven to 450 degrees. Coat a regular-size foil oven bag or a large piece of foil with nonstick cooking spray and place in a shallow baking pan.
2. Cook the orzo in boiling water in a saucepan for 5 minutes. Drain.
3. Place the orzo in large bowl. Add 1 teaspoon of the olive oil, the tomatoes, green onions, cheese, lemon zest, lemon juice, salt and pepper. Gently mix together.
4. Place the orzo mixture in the prepared oven bag.
5. Combine the shrimp and basil in a bowl. Arrange the shrimp mixture on top of the orzo mixture.
6. Fold the edge of the bag over to seal. Bake for 25 minutes or until the shrimp are done. Cut open the bag and drizzle the shrimp with the remaining 1 teaspoon olive oil.

Prep Time: 20 minutes   Cook Time: 25 minutes   Yield: 2 servings

Halibut with Rock Shrimp Salsa

Tobiano is an eclectic restaurant with an open-air kitchen in downtown Steamboat Springs. It has an ever-changing menu that reflects Chef Richie's devotion to a creative, culinary experience.

CHEF RICHIE BILLINGHAM

FRESH TOMATO SALSA
   (Yield: 1 cup)
1 tablespoon olive oil
1/2 onion, minced
1 tablespoon chopped garlic
1 pickled jalapeño chile,
   seeded and minced
1 cup coarsely chopped
   peeled tomatoes
   (about 2 medium)
1 tablespoon coarsely
   chopped cilantro
1 tablespoon fresh lime juice
1 tablespoon roasted chile oil
1/4 teaspoon cumin
20 turns ground white pepper
2 ounces tequila

HALIBUT AND SHRIMP
4 fresh halibut fillets
   (5 ounces each)
Salt and freshly ground
   white pepper to taste
Flour
3 tablespoons olive oil
8 ounces rock shrimp
1 cup Fresh Tomato Salsa
2 tablespoons tequila
1 tablespoon cold butter
Fresh cilantro sprigs
Avocado slices
Grilled and buttered flour
   tortillas, chopped

FOR THE SALSA:

1. Heat the olive oil in a medium skillet over medium heat. Add the onion. Cook for 10 minutes or until nicely caramelized, stirring occasionally. Add the garlic to the skillet. Cook for 2 to 3 minutes longer or until the garlic is brown.
2. Combine the onion mixture, jalapeño chile, tomatoes, cilantro, lime juice, chile oil, cumin, white pepper and tequila in a small bowl. Set aside.

FOR THE HALIBUT:

1. Season the halibut with salt and white pepper. Lightly dust with flour.
2. Heat the olive oil in a sauté pan over medium heat. Sauté the halibut in the hot oil for 5 to 6 minutes or until light brown. Turn fish over and brown for 2 minutes. Add the rock shrimp and salsa. Cook over medium heat for about 1 to 2 minutes while the salsa boils. Add the tequila. Remove from the heat and ignite with a long match. Let stand until the flame subsides. Stir in the butter. Hold in a warm oven for 5 to 10 minutes.
3. To serve, spoon salsa in the center of a plate. Set the halibut fillet on top. Garnish with cilantro, avocado slices and tortillas.

Prep Time: 30 minutes   Cook Time: 10 minutes   Yield: 4 servings

Trout with Brown Butter & Capers

Get a kick out of the popped capers.

¹/₄ cup all-purpose flour
¹/₄ cup yellow cornmeal
1 teaspoon salt
¹/₂ teaspoon freshly ground pepper
4 boned trout fillets (6 to 7 ounces each)
¹/₂ cup (1 stick) butter, divided
2 tablespoons capers, drained
Lemon wedges
Chopped parsley

1. Mix the flour, cornmeal, salt and pepper on a large shallow plate.
2. Rinse the trout and pat dry. Dredge the trout in the flour mixture, coating well on both sides.
3. Melt 3 tablespoons of the butter in a 12-inch nonstick skillet over high heat. Place 2 trout fillets skin side down in the skillet and cook for about 2 minutes or until brown. Reduce the heat to medium. Turn the fish and cook for about 2 minutes longer or until done. Remove to heated dinner plates.
4. Add 3 tablespoons of the remaining butter to the skillet and cook the remaining two fillets in the same manner. Remove to heated dinner plates.
5. Melt the remaining 2 tablespoons butter in the skillet. Add the capers. Cook for about 1 to 2 minutes or until the capers pop open and the butter is brown, shaking the skillet frequently.
6. Spoon the caper butter over the fish. Garnish with lemon wedges and parsley.

Prep Time: 5 minutes   Cook Time: 10 minutes   Yield: 4 servings

Tuna Tofu Bake

Real comfort food! Reminiscent of tuna casserole with the healthy addition of tofu. This soufflé-like main dish is also very good cold and sliced for sandwiches.

MUSICIAN CARY LEWIS

1-pound tofu, drained and cut into ¹/₂ inch cubes
1 small can tuna
³/₄ cup mayonnaise
2 tablespoons onion, grated
2 tablespoons lemon juice
¹/₂ cup (2 ounces) grated Cheddar cheese
Pepper to taste
¹/₂ cup frozen peas (optional)
¹/₂ cup slivered almonds or other nuts (optional)
¹/₂ cup whole wheat bread crumbs
¹/₄ cup wheat germ
Sunflower seeds or slivered almonds

1. Preheat the oven to 350 degrees.
2. Drain the tuna then flake into a large bowl. Stir the mayonnaise, onion, lemon juice, cheese, pepper, peas and almonds into the tuna and blend well.
3. Carefully fold in tofu cubes to avoid crushing them. Spoon mixture into a 2- or 3-quart soufflé dish or flat baking dish.
4. Sprinkle the top with bread crumbs and wheat germ. Sprinkle with additional cheese, if desired, and a handful of sunflower seeds.
5. Bake about 45 minutes or until brown and puffy. Serve immediately.

Prep Time: 17 minutes   Cook Time: 45 minutes   Yield: 4 to 6 servings

Cary Lewis is in constant demand as a collaborative pianist for soloists and chamber music groups. He is a member of the Lanier Trio with his wife, Dorothy, and their recording of the complete Dvorak Trios was honored by Time Magazine as one of the 10 best music recordings of 1993.

Lamb & Red Pepper Ragu with Pasta

Lamb offers a remarkably subtle flavor to this delicate pasta dish.

1 pound ground lamb
1 tablespoon olive oil
1 red onion, chopped
1 yellow bell pepper, chopped
1 red bell pepper, chopped
3 garlic cloves, minced
1 cup red wine
1 cup canned crushed tomatoes
3 tablespoons chopped fresh parsley
1 teaspoon salt
$^{1}/_{2}$ teaspoon crushed red pepper
4 bay leaves
1 can (14$^{1}/_{2}$ ounces) chicken broth
8 cups cooked penne (about 1 pound)
$^{3}/_{4}$ cup grated fresh Parmesan cheese

1. Place the lamb and olive oil in a large Dutch oven. Cook over medium heat for 5 to 6 minutes or until brown, stirring and breaking the lamb into small pieces. Remove and keep warm.
2. Add the onion, bell peppers and garlic to the Dutch oven and sauté until brown. Add a little more oil if necessary. Reduce the heat. Cover and cook for 10 to 12 minutes, stirring occasionally.
3. Return the lamb to the Dutch oven and add the wine. Bring to a boil and cook for 10 minutes to reduce the liquid.
4. Add the tomatoes, parsley, salt, red pepper, bay leaves and chicken broth. Bring to a boil. Reduce the heat and simmer for 10 minutes.
5. Discard the bay leaves. Add the pasta and toss to coat. Gradually add the cheese and toss after each addition.

Prep Time: 30 minutes   Cook Time: 40 minutes   Yield: 8 servings

Lasagna of Roasted Butternut Squash

A great vegetarian entrée, rich and satisfying.

3 pounds butternut squash, quartered, peeled and diced
3 tablespoons olive oil or canola oil
Salt to taste
4 cups milk
2 tablespoons dried rosemary, crumbled
1 tablespoon minced garlic
1/4 cup (1/2 stick) butter

1/4 cup all-purpose flour
Freshly ground pepper to taste
9 sheets (1/2x3x7-inch) dry no-bake lasagna noodles
1 1/3 cups (about 5 ounces) freshly grated Parmesan cheese
1 cup heavy whipping cream
1/2 teaspoon salt
Rosemary sprigs for garnish

1. Preheat the oven to 450 degrees. Oil 2 large rimmed baking sheets.
2. Toss the squash and olive oil together in a large bowl to coat the squash. Spread the squash in a single layer on the baking sheets and place in the oven. Bake for 10 minutes. Season with salt. Stir the squash and bake for 15 minutes longer or until tender and beginning to turn golden brown. Remove from the oven.
3. Mix the milk and rosemary in a saucepan and bring to a simmer over medium heat. Reduce the heat to low and simmer for 10 minutes. Strain the milk mixture through a fine sieve into a pitcher or large measuring cup.
4. Cook the garlic and butter in a large heavy skillet over medium-low heat until softened. Stir in the flour and cook for 3 minutes, stirring constantly. Remove from the heat and whisk in the milk mixture in a slow stream until smooth. Return the skillet to the heat and simmer the sauce for about 10 minutes, stirring occasionally.
5. Add the cooked squash, salt and pepper. Can be prepared ahead and refrigerated at this point.
6. Reduce the oven temperature to 375 degrees. Grease a 9x13-inch glass or ceramic baking dish.
7. Beat the cream and salt in a bowl with an electric mixer until it holds soft peaks.
8. Layer 1 cup of the sauce, 1/3 of the lasagna sheets (no overlapping or touching), 1/2 of the remaining sauce, 1/2 cup of the cheese, 1/3 of the lasagna sheets, the remaining sauce, 1/2 cup of the cheese, the remaining lasagna sheets, all the cream mixture and the remaining cheese in the baking dish.
9. Cover the baking dish with foil, tenting if necessary so that the foil does not touch the cream layer.
10. Bake for 35 minutes. Remove the foil and bake for 10 to 15 minutes longer or until bubbling and golden brown. Let stand for 5 minutes before serving. Garnish with rosemary sprigs.

Prep Time: 1 1/4 hours   Cook Time: 50 minutes

Yield: 6 servings, 12 side dish servings

Carrot & Sweet Potato Purée

The food processor makes fast work of this easy, fall side dish.

4 large sweet potatoes (about 2 pounds)
1 pound carrots
1 tablespoon sugar (optional)
$^1/_2$ cup (1 stick) butter, softened
Salt and pepper to taste
$^1/_2$ cup sour cream
$^1/_2$ teaspoon grated nutmeg

1. Preheat the oven to 400 degrees.
2. Scrub the potatoes and cut a slit in the tops. Place in an 8x10-inch baking pan. Bake for 1 hour and 15 minutes or until tender. Let stand for 10 to 15 minutes or until cool enough to handle.
3. Peel and trim the carrots. Cut into 1-inch pieces. Place in a saucepan and cover with water. Add the sugar. Bring to a boil and cook, covered, for about 30 minutes or until tender. Drain the carrots and add the butter.
4. Place the carrot mixture and the sweet potato pulp in a food processor. Add the sour cream and process until very smooth.
5. Add the nutmeg and more salt and pepper if necessary.
6. Pour into an ovenproof dish. Refrigerate if not serving immediately.
7. To reheat, bake, covered, at 350 degrees for 25 minutes or until hot.

Prep Time: 20 minutes   Cook Time: 1 hour, 15 minutes

Reheat Time: 25 minutes   Yield: 8 servings

Stuffed Zucchini

Anyone who grows zucchini knows that sometimes there is an overabundance, even in Steamboat. This recipe makes great use of this versatile vegetable.

6 zucchini
1 1/2 cups (6 ounces) shredded sharp Cheddar cheese
1/2 cup small curd cottage cheese
2 eggs, lightly beaten
1 tablespoon chopped parsley
2 tablespoons chopped onion
Salt and pepper to taste
1/2 cup dry bread crumbs
2 tablespoons butter, melted

1. Preheat the oven to 350 degrees.
2. Cut the zucchini into halves lengthwise. Steam for 5 to 6 minutes or until slightly tender. Remove and discard the seeds. Pat the zucchini dry.
3. Combine the cheeses, eggs, parsley, onion, salt and pepper and mix well.
4. Stuff the zucchini shells with filling and place in a large baking dish.
5. Combine the bread crumbs and butter and sprinkle over the zucchini.
6. Bake for 30 minutes.

Prep Time: 15 minutes   Cook Time: 30 minutes
Yield: 12 side servings, 6 entrée servings

It seems as though it happens overnight. One autumn day you are wondering when the foliage will be at its peak, and then suddenly, it is! Steamboat Springs has more than its fair share of aspen. Signature gold leaves are part of a medley of colors–a virtual symphony of red, orange, yellow and green. Favorite summer trails are transformed into an entirely new experience, a memory to cherish into the winter.

Orzo with Mushrooms

*Orzo is a small oval pasta, often mistaken for rice, that
has its own distinctive texture and flavor.*

1 1/3 cups orzo
2 tablespoons butter
3 cups sliced fresh mushrooms
4 large green onions, chopped
1/2 teaspoon pepper
1/4 teaspoon salt
2 garlic cloves, minced
1/2 cup water
1/2 teaspoon marjoram
1 teaspoon instant chicken bouillon granule,s or
    1 chicken bouillon cube
Grated Parmesan cheese

1. Cook the orzo using the package directions; drain.
2. Melt the butter in a large skillet over medium heat. Stir in the mushrooms, green
   onions, pepper, salt and garlic. Cook for 5 minutes.
3. Add the water, marjoram and bouillon granules. Reduce the heat and cook for
   about 6 minutes or until the liquid is almost absorbed.
4. Toss the mushroom mixture with the pasta in a bowl. Sprinkle with cheese.
5. Serve immediately.

To keep mushrooms from turning brown, store them in a brown paper bag or paper
towel in the refrigerator.

Prep Time: 15 minutes   Cook Time: 20 to 22 minutes   Yield: 6 servings

Sesame Soba Noodles with Asparagus

Soba noodles, made from buckwheat flours, are an Asian staple.
Here, their hearty flavor balances the delicacy of asparagus.

1 1/2 pounds asparagus, trimmed
1 pound soba noodles (available in Asian
    section of most supermarkets)
1/4 cup dark sesame oil
1/2 cup julienned red bell pepper
1/8 cup chopped green onions
1 teaspoon black sesame seeds
2 tablespoons soy sauce

1. Cook the asparagus in boiling water in a saucepan for about 1 minute. Plunge into ice water to stop the cooking process. Cut into 2-inch pieces.
2. Boil the noodles in a saucepan for about 7 minutes or until just past al dente. Drain.
3. Add sesame oil to the noodles. Toss the asparagus, bell pepper and green onions with the noodles. Sprinkle with the sesame seeds and soy sauce.
4. Can be served hot or cold.

Prep Time: 10 minutes   Yield: 12 servings

There has always been a connection between the festival and local visual artists. One piece of art is selected each season and featured on the festival program cover as well as on posters and tee shirts. A silent auction for this original art is conducted throughout the season, and the winner is announced at the season's finale. Now almost collectors' items, these various images can be seen on tee shirts and on the walls of Strings patrons throughout the country

Quinoa (pronounced keen-wa) is an ancient grain dating back to the Inca civilization in South America. It is a complete protein grain, which the National Academy of Sciences calls "one of the best sources of protein in the vegetable kingdom." It is quick and easy to prepare, tasty, easy to digest, and even gluten free. Use it in any way you would rice or pasta.

Quinoa Mexican Bake

Try this versatile and nutritious grain as a side dish with any entrée.

4 cups cooked quinoa
1 small onion, chopped
1 tomato, chopped
1 can (4 ounces) chopped green chiles
3/4 cup sour cream or low-fat plain yogurt
1/2 cup chopped green bell pepper

1 can (15 ounces) black beans or sliced olives
1/2 cup corn
1 cup (4 ounces) shredded sharp Cheddar cheese,
1 package (4 ounces) goat cheese crumbles
Salt and freshly ground pepper to taste

1. Preheat the oven to 375 degrees.
2. Combine all the ingredients in a medium bowl and mix well.
3. Pour into an 8x8-inch baking dish. Bake for 45 minutes.

Prep Time: 20 minutes   Cook Time: 45 minutes   Yield: 4 servings

Wild Rice Pilaf

The sweetness of apple juice and fruit makes this a harmonious accompaniment to poultry or pork entrées.

1 cup chopped onion
1 cup chopped celery
2 tablespoons butter
2 1/2 cups wild rice, rinsed and drained
1 1/2 cups chicken broth
2 1/2 cups apple cider or apple juice

1/2 cup slivered almonds, toasted
1/4 cup dried cherries, cranberries or apricots
1/3 cup minced parsley
Salt and pepper

1. Sauté the onion and celery in the butter in a large saucepan for about 10 minutes or until light brown.
2. Stir in the wild rice, chicken broth and apple cider. Bring to a boil. Cover and reduce the heat. Simmer for 1 1/4 to 1 1/2 hours or until the grains begin to split and the rice is tender. Drain any liquid.
3. Stir almonds, cherries and parsley into the rice. Season with salt and pepper.

Prep Time: 25 minutes   Cook Time: 1 1/4 to 1 1/2 hours   Yield: 8 to10 servings

Basil Pine Nut Biscotti

This savory version of biscotti is great with soup or salad.

3/4 cup pine nuts
2 cups all-purpose flour
1/2 cup (2 ounces) grated Parmesan cheese
2 teaspoons baking powder
2 teaspoons basil, crumbled
1 teaspoon grated lemon zest
1/2 teaspoon salt
6 tablespoons butter, cut into small pieces
1/4 cup nonfat milk
2 eggs

1. Preheat the oven to 350 degrees. Oil a 12x15-inch cookie sheet.
2. Bake the pine nuts on a small baking pan or baking sheet for about 10 minutes or until light brown. Set aside.
3. Mix the flour, cheese, baking powder, basil, lemon zest and salt in a large bowl. Cut in the butter with a pastry blender or fork until the crumbs of butter are the size of small peas or smaller. Add the pine nuts.
4. Blend the milk and eggs in a medium bowl. Add to the flour mixture and stir gently with a wooden spoon until the dough forms a ball.
5. Shape the dough on the baking sheet into a rectangle about 15 inches long and 1 inch thick. Bake for 15 to 17 minutes. Remove from the oven.
6. Gently slice diagonally into 1-inch-wide slices while still on the baking sheet. The greater the angle you cut, the longer the biscotti will be. Place the slices on a cut edge on the oiled baking sheet and return to the oven.
7. Reduce the oven temperature to 325 degrees. Bake for 50 to 55 minutes longer or until the biscotti are light brown, dry and firm to the touch.
8. Cool on wire racks. Serve slightly warm or wrap airtight when completely cool to serve later or freeze.

 For lower altitudes, bake in step 5 for 15 minutes.
Bake in step 7 for 40 to 50 minutes.

Prep Time: 20 minutes   Cook Time: 65 to 70 minutes   Yield: 16 to 18 pieces

Fruit Coffee Cake

Celebrate the abundance of seasonal fruits in this morning treat.

2 cups sifted all-purpose flour
$^1/_2$ teaspoon salt
$^1/_2$ cup sugar
4 teaspoons baking powder
$^1/_4$ cup butter
1 egg
1 cup milk
2 or 3 small apples, pears or peaches
$^1/_4$ cup sugar
2 teaspoons cinnamon

1. Preheat the oven to 450 degrees. Grease a 7x11-inch baking pan or 9-inch deep-dish pie plate.
2. Mix the flour, salt, sugar and baking powder in a large bowl. Cut in the butter.
3. Beat the egg and milk together in a small bowl. Stir into the flour mixture just until moistened. A food processor works well for steps 2 and 3.
4. Pour into the pan. Let the dough stand while preparing the fruit.
5. Peel and core the fruit. Lay thin overlapping slices on top of the dough. Sprinkle the sugar and cinnamon over the top.
6. Bake for 25 to 35 minutes or until a toothpick inserted in the center comes out clean.

Prep Time: 30 minutes   Cook Time: 25 to 35 minutes   Yield: 1 coffee cake

Although best used fresh, peaches may be frozen when ripe. Peel and cut into halves onto a plastic wrap-lined cookie sheet. Place cookie sheet in freezer for several hours, then place the individually frozen peach halves in a freezer bag. Use in cobblers, crisps, or smoothies.

Chai Muffins

If you love the flavor of spicy chai tea, you'll love these muffins.
Enjoy for breakfast, a snack, or lunch with cheese.

1 cup unbleached
  all-purpose flour
1 cup whole wheat flour
1/2 teaspoon salt
1 1/2 teaspoons
  baking powder
1/2 teaspoon cinnamon
1/2 teaspoon cloves
1/2 teaspoon cardamom
1/2 teaspoon ginger
3/4 cup milk
1/2 cup honey

1/4 cup plus 2 tablespoon
  canola oil
1 teaspoon vanilla extract
1 extra-large egg
1/2 to 1 cup chopped walnuts
1/2 cup golden raisins
  (optional)
About 1 tablespoon sugar
  mixed with a pinch of
  cloves and ginger for
  topping

1. Preheat the oven to 400 degrees. Grease or line a muffin pan with muffin papers (12-cup for regular-size and 24-cup for miniature).
2. Combine the flours, salt, baking powder, cinnamon, cloves, cardamom and ginger in a large bowl. Stir to blend well.
3. Mix the milk, honey, canola oil, vanilla and egg in a medium bowl. Whisk to blend well.
4. Add the wet ingredients to the dry ingredients. Add the walnuts and raisins, stirring only enough to blend. Do not overmix. Pour or spoon into the prepared muffin pan, filling each about 3/4 full. Sprinkle the tops with the sugar and spice mixture.
5. Bake for 18 minutes for regular muffins or 12 to 14 minutes for miniature muffins, or until a toothpick inserted in the center comes out clean.
6. Let cool in pans for 5 to 10 minutes and then turn out onto a wire rack to cool completely.

At sea level, increase the baking powder to 2 teaspoons and reduce the egg to 1 large; reduce the cooking time by about 5 minutes for regular-size and 2 to 3 minutes for miniatures.

Prep Time: 15 minutes

Cook Time: 18 minutes for regular, 12 to 14 minutes for miniature

Yield: 12 regular muffins, 24 miniature muffins

You know you're in a small town when the main street shuts down for trick-or-treating. Costume-clad kids and families stroll door-to-door collecting treats from downtown businesses. You can depend on it being frigid and probably snowy, but nearly the entire town turns out for this popular community happening regardless of the weather.

Double-Chocolate Brownies

For chocoholics everywhere.

2 squares (1 ounce each) unsweetened chocolate
$^1/_2$ cup (1 stick) butter
2 extra-large eggs
$^3/_4$ cup sugar
1 teaspoon vanilla extract or almond extract
$^1/_2$ cup all-purpose flour
$^1/_8$ teaspoon salt
1 cup chopped walnuts (optional)
$^1/_2$ cup semisweet chocolate pieces
   (or white chocolate chips)

1. Preheat the oven to 375 degrees. Grease a 9x9-inch or 7x11-inch baking pan.
2. Melt the chocolate squares and butter in a small saucepan or in a microwave-safe bowl in the microwave, stirring periodically during the melting process as butter melts faster than chocolate.
3. Beat the eggs until thick and pale yellow in a bowl. Gradually beat in the sugar until the mixture is thick and fluffy. Stir in the chocolate mixture and vanilla. Blend in the flour and salt. Fold in the walnuts and semisweet chocolate pieces.
4. Pour into the pan. Bake for 25 minutes or until a shiny top crust forms.
5. Cool completely in the pan on a wire rack. Loosen around the edges with a sharp knife. Cut into 16 squares and remove from the pan.

Serving Suggestion: Ice cream or whipped cream is a good accompaniment.

At sea level, use 2 large eggs and 1 cup sugar. Bake at 350 degrees.

Prep Time: 20 minutes   Cook Time: 25 minutes   Yield: 16 bars

Nanaimo Bars

Indulge in this popular Canadian classic.

BASE
1/2 cup (1 stick) butter,
  softened
1/4 cup sugar
5 tablespoons unsweetened
  baking cocoa
1 teaspoon vanilla extract
1 egg
2 cups graham cracker
  crumbs
1 cup unsweetened coconut
  (available in health food
  stores)
1/2 cup chopped walnuts

ICING
1/4 cup (1/2 stick) butter
2 cups confectioners' sugar
2 tablespoons vanilla
  custard powder (available
  at most supermarkets
  in pudding mix section)
2 to 3 tablespoons milk

GLAZE
3/4 cup chocolate chips
4 ounces semisweet
  chocolate squares
2 tablespoons butter

FOR THE BASE:
1. Place the butter, sugar, baking cocoa, vanilla and egg in a bowl. Set the bowl over a pan of boiling water, making sure the bottom of the bowl is not resting on the bottom of the pan. Stir until the butter has melted and the mixture is the consistency of custard. You can also use a double boiler for this step.
2. Mix the graham cracker crumbs, coconut and walnuts. Stir into the cocoa mixture.
3. Pack into an ungreased 9x9-inch baking pan. Chill in the refrigerator.

FOR THE ICING:
1. Cream the butter, confectioners' sugar and custard powder in a bowl with an electric mixer. Add the milk and beat until smooth.
2. Spread the icing over the cooled base and let stand or refrigerate for 1 hour.

FOR THE GLAZE:
1. Melt the chocolates and butter in a bowl over hot water. You can also use a double boiler for this step. Mix well and then spread on top of the icing.
2. Refrigerate to harden (about 30 minutes). Cut into squares before the chocolate becomes too hard.

Prep Time: 1 hour   Cool Time: 1 1/2 hours   Yield: 16 bars (1 1/2 inch squares)

Shortbread Cookies

These buttery treats will become your family's favorites.

1 cup (2 sticks) butter, softened
1/2 cup granulated sugar
2 cups all-purpose flour
1 cup confectioners' sugar
1 teaspoon vanilla powder

1. Cream the butter in a food processor mixing bowl. Blend in the granulated sugar. Cut in the flour until crumbly. Turn into a bowl and knead until smooth.
2. Divide the dough into fourths and shape into cylindrical rolls, approximately 1 inch in diameter and 5 inches long. Wrap in plastic wrap and refrigerate for several hours. It can be frozen at this point.
3. Preheat the oven to 300 degrees.
4. Mix the confectioners' sugar and vanilla powder in a bowl and set aside.
5. Cut the rolls into 1/4-inch slices and place on an ungreased cookie sheet.
6. Bake at 300 degrees for 25 minutes or until light golden brown on the edges.
7. Let stand for a few minutes and then roll the warm cookies in the confectioners' sugar mixture. Cool on wire racks.

♪ If vanilla powder is not found in the spice section at your supermarket, you can make your own vanilla sugar. Split a vanilla bean in half and scrape the seeds into 1 cup confectioners' sugar. Add the bean halves and store in an airtight container for at least 24 hours. To use, remove the bean halves and stir the sugar to evenly distribute the vanilla flavor. Substitute this sugar for the combined sugar and vanilla powder.

Prep Time: 30 minutes   Chill Time: 2 hours   Cook Time: 25 minutes per batch

Yield: 4 to 5 dozen

Cinnamon Apple Cake

Enjoy the essence of apple pie in this rich, moist cake.

1³/₄ cups sugar, divided
³/₄ cup (6 ounces) block-style fat-free
  cream cheese, softened
¹/₂ cup (1 stick) butter, softened
1 teaspoon vanilla extract
2 eggs
1¹/₂ cups all-purpose flour
1¹/₂ teaspoons baking powder
¹/₄ teaspoon salt
2 teaspoons cinnamon
3 cups chopped peeled Rome apples
  (about 2 large)

1. Preheat the oven to 350 degrees. Spray an 8-inch springform pan with nonstick
   cooking spray.
2. Beat 1¹/₂ cups of the sugar, the cream cheese, butter and vanilla in a bowl at
   medium speed for about 4 minutes or until well blended. Add the eggs one at a
   time, beating well after each addition. Set aside.
3. Mix the flour, baking powder and salt in a bowl. Add the flour mixture to the
   creamed mixture and beat at low speed until blended.
4. Combine the remaining ¹/₄ cup sugar and cinnamon in a small bowl. Mix
   2 tablespoons of the cinnamon mixture and the chopped apples in a bowl. Stir
   the apple mixture into the cake batter.
5. Pour the batter into the prepared pan and sprinkle with the remaining
   cinnamon mixture.
6. Bake at 350 degrees for 1 hour and 15 minutes or until the cake pulls away from
   the side of the pan. Cool the cake completely in the pan on a wire rack.
7. Serve warm with whipped cream or vanilla ice cream.

Prep Time: 20 to 30 minutes   Cook Time: 75 minutes   Yield: 12 servings

Steamboat Carrot Cake

A low-fat carrot cake with all the flavor of the original.

CAKE
1¹/₂ cups unbleached all-
   purpose flour
1 cup whole wheat flour
2 teaspoons cinnamon
1¹/₄ teaspoons baking powder
1¹/₄ teaspoons baking soda
¹/₂ teaspoon salt
1¹/₄ cups packed brown sugar
1 can (20 ounces) crushed
   pineapple, drained well
3 extra-large eggs
³/₄ cup low-fat buttermilk
¹/₂ cup unsweetened
   applesauce
¹/₃ cup canola oil
2 teaspoons vanilla extract

3 cups lightly packed grated
   carrots
¹/₂ cup chopped walnuts
¹/₂ cup sweetened flaked
   coconut

FROSTING
8 ounces low-fat cream
   cheese, softened
3 cups confectioners' sugar,
   sifted
1 teaspoon grated orange zest
1 teaspoon vanilla extract
1 or 2 tablespoons orange
   juice, if needed to moisten
Walnut halves for garnish

FOR THE CAKE:

1. Preheat the oven to 350 degrees. Butter a 9x13-inch cake pan or spray with nonstick cooking spray. For cupcakes, line 3 muffin pans with cupcake liners.
2. Combine the flours, cinnamon, baking powder, baking soda and salt in a medium bowl. Set aside.
3. Beat the brown sugar, pineapple, eggs, buttermilk, applesauce, canola oil and vanilla in a large bowl. Stir in the grated carrot. Add the flour mixture and mix well. Add the walnuts and coconut; stir again. Pour the batter into the prepared cake pan or muffin pans. For cupcakes, do not fill more than ³/₄ full.
4. Bake for 40 to 45 minutes for the cake, or 25 to 30 minutes for the cupcakes, or until a toothpick inserted into the center of the cake or cupcakes comes out clean.
5. Remove from the oven and cool on a wire rack.

FOR THE FROSTING:

1. Mix the cream cheese, confectioners' sugar, orange zest, vanilla and orange juice in a bowl. Spread the frosting on the cooled cake. Decorate each piece or each cupcake with walnut halves, if desired.
2. Store in the refrigerator, covered with plastic wrap, or wrap airtight and freeze.

For lower elevations, increase baking powder and baking soda to 1¹/₂ teaspoons each, increase brown sugar to 1¹/₂ cups, use large eggs, reduce baking time: 35 to 40 minutes for cake, 20 to 25 minutes for cupcakes.

Prep Time: 40 minutes   Cook Time: 40 to 45 minutes cake   Yield: 24 servings

Cook Time: 30 minutes cupcakes   Yield: 36 servings

Cranberry Apple Crisp

Bask in the aromas of this seasonal fruit sensation.

2 cups packed brown sugar, divided
$^1/_2$ cup cornmeal
1 cup old-fashioned oats
$^1/_2$ cup (1 stick) butter, softened
6 large tart green apples, peeled, cored and sliced
1 tablespoon lemon juice
2 cups cranberries, fresh or frozen
　　(cherries can be substituted)
Vanilla ice cream or whipped cream
　　for accompaniment

1. Preheat the oven to 350 degrees.
2. Combine 1 cup brown sugar, the cornmeal and oats in a small bowl. Cut in the butter with a fork or hands until crumbly. Set aside. (It can be made ahead and refrigerated.)
3. Mix the apples with the lemon juice in a 9x13-inch glass baking dish. Add the cranberries and remaining 1 cup brown sugar. Mix well.
4. Sprinkle with the topping mixture, covering the fruit evenly.
5. Bake at 350 degrees for 55 to 60 minutes or until the apples are tender when pierced with a knife, the juices are bubbly and the top is golden brown.
6. Serve warm with ice cream or whipped cream.

Prep Time: 20 minutes　　　Cook Time: 55 to 60 minutes　　　Yield: 6 to 8 servings

The All-American fruit, apples, are abundantly grown in Colorado. The high altitude and climate result in apples with superior color, intense flavor and distinct sweetness. Major varieties include Golden Delicious, Jonagold, Granny Smith, Rome Beauty, and Fuji. For cooking purposes, combine varieties, such as Golden Delicious and Granny Smith, to balance flavor and texture. Always keep apples refrigerated.

Pumpkin Flan

A favorite for Thanksgiving, lighter than pie but still very special.

2/3 cup sugar
2 eggs
3 egg yolks
6 tablespoons sugar
1 cup pumpkin purée
1 teaspoon cinnamon
1/2 teaspoon salt
1/4 teaspoon ginger
1/8 teaspoon nutmeg

1/8 teaspoon ground cloves
1 1/2 cups light cream, scalded (can use fat-free half-and-half or full-strength evaporated milk)
2 tablespoons orange-flavored liqueur (Grand Marnier preferred)

1. Heat a 6-cup soufflé dish in a pan of hot water (save the pan of hot water for cooking the flan later).
2. Heat the sugar in a heavy skillet or saucepan over medium heat for 3 to 5 minutes, watching constantly until the sugar liquefies and turns golden brown. Remove from the heat immediately. Pour the sugar into the heated dish. If the dish is not still hot, the melted sugar will break it. Turn the dish so that the bottom and about 1 inch up the side become coated with the caramel. Set aside.
3. Preheat the oven to 350 degrees.
4. Beat the eggs, egg yolks and sugar in a bowl until foamy. Beat in the pumpkin purée, cinnamon, salt, ginger, nutmeg and cloves. Stir in the scalded cream slowly. Add the liqueur and mix well.
5. Pour the filling into the caramelized dish and place the dish in a pan of hot water so that water comes two-thirds of the way up the sides of the dish.
6. Bake for 1 1/4 hours or until a knife inserted in the center comes out clean.
7. Remove from the oven and remove the dish from the pan of hot water. Let the flan cool at room temperature for 20 minutes and loosen the side with a knife.
8. The flan is ready to serve now or cool in the refrigerator and serve later. Bring to room temperature before serving.
9. Remove the flan from the soufflé dish by placing a serving plate on top and inverting the dish. Scrape out any liquid caramel.

Serving Suggestion: Serve with sweetened whipped cream flavored with additional orange-flavored liqueur.

To scald milk or cream, heat in a saucepan over low heat or in microwave-safe bowl in the microwave to just below boiling.

Prep Time: 20 minutes   Cook Time: 1 1/4 hours   Cool Time: 20 minutes

Yield: 6 servings

Bananas Foster

A popular dessert in the south, this is quick to prepare if you have ice cream and bananas on hand.

3 firm ripe bananas, sliced
   lengthwise and crosswise
2 tablespoons fresh lemon
   juice
4 tablespoons (1/4 cup)
   butter

1/2 cup packed brown sugar
1/4 teaspoon cinnamon
1/3 cup dark rum
2 tablespoons banana
   liqueur
Vanilla ice cream

1. Place the quartered bananas in a shallow bowl and sprinkle with the lemon juice.
2. Melt the butter and brown sugar in a large heavy skillet. Add the banana mixture and heat until syrupy, spooning the sauce over the bananas. Do not overcook. Sprinkle with the cinnamon.
3. Add the rum and banana liqueur and stir into the sauce. Remove from the heat and ignite with a long match, basting the bananas until the flames subside.
4. Serve over ice cream.

   Prep Time: 5 minutes   Cook Time: 5 minutes   Yield: 3 to 4 servings

Bavarian Apple Torte

1/2 cup (1 stick) butter,
   softened
1 cup sugar, divided
1/2 teaspoon vanilla extract,
   divided
1 cup all-purpose flour

1 package (8 ounces) cream
   cheese, softened
1 egg
1/4 teaspoon cinnamon
4 cups sliced peeled
   Granny Smith apples

1. Preheat the oven to 450 degrees. Grease a 9-inch round baking pan.
2. Cream the butter, 1/2 cup of the sugar and 1/4 teaspoon of the vanilla in a bowl. Blend in the flour. Press the mixture onto the bottom and side of the pan, forming a shell.
3. Cream 1/4 cup of the sugar and the cream cheese in a bowl with an electric mixer. Beat the egg and remaining 1/4 teaspoon vanilla in a bowl. Add to the cream cheese mixture. Pour into the unbaked shell.
4. Toss the remaining 1/4 cup sugar, cinnamon and apples in a bowl. Arrange the apple slices over the filling.
5. Bake for 10 minutes. Decrease the oven temperature to 400 degrees. Bake for 20 to 25 minutes longer.

Serving Suggestion: Sprinkle with walnuts, pecans or sliced almonds.

Prep Time: 25 minutes   Cook Time: 30 to 35 minutes   Yield: 8 servings

Winter

Alpenglow bathes Mt. Werner as seen from Campbell Ranch.

Après-Ski Gathering

Roasted Eggplant Spread with Crostini
113

Layered Shrimp
114

Sweet & Sour Meatballs
117

Phyllo Pizza with Three Cheeses
& Tomatoes
120

Hot Cookies
121

Chicken Chili
125

Pesto Corn Bread
158

Chocolate Raspberry Bars With Coconut
161

Chocolate Truffles
171

Formal Dinner

Basil Shrimp Wrapped with Prosciutto
119

Spinach Salad with Avocado,
Oranges, & Feta
130

Beef Tenderloin with Mushroom
& Wine Sauce
132

Garlic Mashed Potatoes
134

Chocolate Soufflés
170

Secret "powder stash" on Mt. Werner.

PHOTOGRAPH BY CHRIS SELBY

Appetizers

Soups & Salads

Entrées

Entrées (continued)

Sides & Accompaniments

Breads

Sweets & Desserts

Roasted Eggplant Spread with Crostini

Roasting the vegetables first enriches the flavor of this spread.

1 eggplant, peeled and cut into 1-inch cubes
2 red bell peppers, cut into 1-inch cubes
1 red onion, peeled and cut into 1-inch cubes
2 garlic cloves, minced
3 tablespoons olive oil
1 1/2 teaspoons kosher salt
1/2 teaspoon freshly ground black pepper
1 tablespoon tomato paste

1. Preheat the oven to 400 degrees.
2. Mix the eggplant, bell peppers, onion, garlic, olive oil, salt and pepper in a large bowl. Spread the mixture on a baking sheet.
3. Bake for 45 minutes or until the vegetables are light brown and soft, tossing once during the cooking. Cool slightly.
4. Place the vegetables in a food processor fitted with a steel blade. Add the tomato paste and pulse 3 or 4 times to blend. Season with additional salt and pepper.
5. Serve with toasted crostini.

Prep Time: 20 minutes   Cook Time: 45 minutes   Yield: 6 to 8 servings

Crostini

1 baguette, sliced crosswise 1/4-inch thick
1/4 cup extra-virgin olive oil

1. Preheat the oven to 350 degrees.
2. Arrange the baguette slices on baking sheets and brush with olive oil.
3. Bake for 15 minutes or until toasted.
4. Once cooled, the crostini can be stored overnight in an airtight tin. Recrisp in a preheated 350-degree oven before serving.

Prep Time: 5 minutes   Cook Time: 15 minutes   Yield: 30 crostini

Layered Shrimp

A colorful favorite at any gathering.

1 package (8 ounces) cream cheese, softened
2 garlic cloves, minced
1 teaspoon Worcestershire sauce
1 1/2 teaspoons Tabasco sauce
12 ounces shrimp, peeled, deveined and cooked
6 ounces cocktail sauce or seafood sauce
4 ounces mozzarella cheese, shredded
4 green onions, chopped
1/2 bell pepper, chopped
1 tomato, chopped
2 tablespoons grated Parmesan cheese

1. Mix the cream cheese, garlic, Worcestershire sauce and Tabasco sauce in a bowl. Spread the mixture on a 10- or 12-inch platter.
2. Layer the shrimp, cocktail sauce, mozzarella cheese, green onions, bell pepper, tomato and Parmesan cheese in the order listed.
3. Refrigerate for 24 hours.
4. Serve with crackers.

Prep Time: 20 minutes   Chill Time: 24 hours   Yield: 10 servings

Elk & Cherry Tartare

While most tartares are made raw, in this recipe from La Montaña,
the elk loin is grilled until rare, then diced into small cubes.

CHEF DAMON RENFROE

1 1/2 pounds fresh elk short loin (have butcher remove
   all silver skin)
Salt and pepper to taste
1/2 cup sun-dried cherries, rehydrated in water or brandy
3 tablespoons capers, drained and chopped
1/4 cup finely diced roasted red bell peppers
1/2 cup minced red onion
1 bunch cilantro, chopped
1/3 cup Chipotle Remoulade (see page 180)
Field greens for garnish
1/2 bag blue corn tortilla chips

1. Preheat the grill.
2. Season the cleaned elk loin pieces with salt and pepper. Grill until rare, about
    2 minutes per side. Let cool. Dice the elk into 1/4-inch cubes. Place in a mixing bowl.
3. Chop the rehydrated cherries into small pieces. Add the cherries, capers, red
    peppers, onion and cilantro to the elk and mix well. Add the Chipotle Rémoulade
    and mix well.
4. Place field greens on a serving platter. Mold the elk tartare in the center of the
    platter, on top of the field greens. Arrange blue corn tortilla chips around the tartare.

Prep Time: 30 minutes   Cook Time: 4 minutes   Yield: 6 to 15 appetizers

Argentine Empanadas

Each region of Argentina is proud of its empanadas, and these are similar to what you would enjoy in a typical restaurant in Buenos Aires.

MUSICIAN RALPH J. VOTAPEK

Ralph Votapek is the Gold Medalist of the first Van Cliburn International Piano Competition and winner of the prestigious Naumburg Award. He has performed throughout the world and appeared as soloist with hundreds of orchestras.

3/4 pounds ground beef
1 large garlic clove, minced
1 onion, chopped
1/2 cup chopped raisins
1/2 teaspoon chili powder
1/4 teaspoon cumin
Few drops of Tabasco sauce
1 1/2 teaspoons
   all-purpose flour

1 1/2 teaspoons capers,
   drained
1 tablespoon tomato paste
3/4 teaspoon sugar
1 package (17 ounces)
   puff pastry sheets
1/4 to 1/2 cup sliced
   green olives
2 egg yolks, beaten

1. Brown the ground beef in a skillet, stirring until crumbly; drain well. Add the garlic and onion. Cook until the onion is translucent. Stir in the raisins, chili powder, cumin, Tabasco sauce, flour, capers, tomato paste and sugar. Add a little water if the mixture seems dry.
2. Preheat the oven to 375 degrees.
3. Roll out each pastry sheet into a 14-inch square. Cut into nine 5-inch circles. Fill each circle with a heaping tablespoon of the meat mixture and an olive slice. Moisten the edges with the eggs, fold over and seal. Crimp with a fork or with fingers to seal tightly. Brush lightly with the eggs and place on an ungreased baking sheet.
4. Bake for 15 to 20 minutes or until lightly browned.

♪ To make bite-size empanadas, cut the pastry into thirty-two 3-inch circles. Place heaping teaspoon of the filling on each circle. The filling can be frozen for several months.

Prep Time: 1 hour   Cook Time: 20 minutes   Yield: 18 large or 32 small

Sweet & Sour Meatballs

Appetizer meatballs are a perennial crowd-pleaser.

MEATBALLS
1 pound ground beef
1 egg
1 tablespoon cornstarch
2 tablespoons chopped
   onion
1 teaspoon salt
1/4 teaspoon pepper

SAUCE
3/4 cup sugar
3 tablespoons cornstarch
1/4 cup soy sauce
1/3 cup cider vinegar
2/3 cup water

FOR THE MEATBALLS:
1. Preheat the oven to 350 degrees. Combine the ground beef, egg, cornstarch, onion, salt and pepper in a bowl and mix well.
2. Shape into 1-inch balls and place on a rimmed baking sheet. Bake for 30 minutes. Remove to a ceramic fondue pot.

FOR THE SAUCE:
1. Mix the sugar and cornstarch in a medium saucepan. Add the soy sauce, vinegar and water, stirring until smooth. Cook over low heat for 4 to 5 minutes or until the mixture thickens, stirring constantly.
2. Pour the sauce over the meatballs. Serve warm.

Prep Time: 15 minutes   Cook Time: 30 minutes   Yield: 18 to 20 (1-inch) meatballs

Sausage-Stuffed Mushrooms

3 hot Italian sausages (about 10 ounces),
    casings removed, chopped
1 1/2 teaspoons oregano
1 cup (4 ounces) grated Parmesan cheese, divided
1/2 teaspoon Worcestershire sauce
1/2 teaspoon garlic powder
1 package (8 ounces) cream cheese, softened
Salt and pepper to taste
24 to 36 large mushrooms, stemmed

1. Preheat the oven to 350 degrees. Oil a 10x15-inch baking pan.
2. Sauté the sausage and oregano in a skillet over medium-high heat until brown. Remove to a large bowl using a slotted spoon. Let cool. Mix in 1/2 cup of the Parmesan cheese, Worcestershire sauce and garlic powder. Stir in the cream cheese, salt and pepper.
3. Fill the mushroom caps with the sausage filling and sprinkle with the remaining Parmesan cheese.
4. Bake for about 25 minutes.

Prep Time: 30 minutes   Cook Time: 25 to 30 minutes   Yield: 24 to 36 servings

In the 1860s, French fur trappers stopping in the area were startled to hear the sound of a steamboat on the Yampa River. Upon investigation, they discovered the chugging sound came from a nearby hot spring that they named Steamboat Spring. The name Steamboat Springs was subsequently given to the developing town.

Basil Shrimp Wrapped with Prosciutto

An unusual and delicious combination of flavors and textures.

CHEF DAVID NELSON

1 teaspoon minced garlic
1 tablespoon olive oil
1/8 teaspoon peppercorns, cracked
20 shrimp (41- to 50-count), peeled (leave tail on)
  and deveined
2 to 3 ounces (10 slices) prosciutto, each slice
  cut lengthwise into 2 strips
8 large fresh basil leaves, each cut into 2- to 3-inch strips
Dipping Sauce (see recipe below)

1. Mix the garlic, olive oil and peppercorns in a bowl. Add the shrimp and marinate for 30 minutes at room temperature.
2. Soak bamboo skewers for 30 minutes.
3. Place the prosciutto slices on a work surface. Layer each slice with a strip of basil and 1 shrimp. Roll up and thread shrimp pieces onto the soaked skewers.
4. Preheat the grill. Preheat the oven to 350 degrees.
5. Grill the kabobs for 3 to 5 minutes or until the fat on the prosciutto is cooked off, turning frequently. (Be careful; the prosciutto will flare up.) Bake in the oven for 4 to 5 minutes longer.
6. Serve with dipping sauce on the side.

Prep Time: 10 minutes   Stand Time: 30 minutes   Cook Time: 10 minutes

Yield: 20 pieces

Dipping Sauce

1/8 cup red wine vinegar
1 tablespoon Dijon mustard
2 teaspoons minced garlic
1 teaspoon chopped fresh basil
1/2 cup olive oil
Salt and pepper to taste

Place the vinegar, mustard, garlic and basil in a blender. Pulse a few times. With blender running at high speed, slowly add the olive oil in a fine stream until the sauce is thick like mayonnaise. Season with salt and pepper. Chill.

Prep Time: 10 minutes   Yield: 3/4 cup

Phyllo Pizza with Three Cheeses & Tomatoes

Working with phyllo is fun, and the results are always admired and appreciated.

CHEF CLYDE NELSON

10 sheets phyllo dough
3 tablespoons butter
3 tablespoons olive oil
$^{1}/_{2}$ cup (3 ounces) feta cheese, finely crumbled
$^{1}/_{2}$ cup (2 ounces) shredded mozzarella cheese
$^{1}/_{2}$ cup grated Parmesan cheese
1 teaspoon oregano
Salt and freshly ground pepper to taste
4 green onions, sliced
2 large tomatoes, thinly sliced

1. Preheat the oven to 400 degrees.
2. Cut the sheets of phyllo into 9x14-inch sheets. Place the phyllo on a work surface and cover with a slightly dampened towel.
3. Melt the butter with the olive oil in a small saucepan.
4. Mix the cheeses, oregano, salt and pepper in a bowl.
5. Oil a baking pan with some of the melted butter mixture. Place 1 sheet of phyllo on the pan and brush lightly with the butter mixture. Sprinkle with 2 tablespoons of the cheese mixture. Continue in the same manner until all the phyllo has been used.
6. Brush the top layer with the butter mixture. Layer with half the remaining cheese, the green onions, the tomatoes arranged close together in a single layer, the salt, pepper and the remaining cheese.
7. Trim the edges. Bake on the top rack for 20 to 25 minutes or until the cheese is melted and the phyllo is golden brown and crisp on the edges.

Prep Time: 30 minutes   Cook Time: 20 to 25 minutes   Yield: 8 to 10 servings

Hot Cookies

The spicy richness of these cookies is sure to awaken anyone's palate.

¹/₂ teaspoon garlic salt
¹/₄ teaspoon cayenne pepper
2 cups all-purpose flour
8 ounces extra-sharp Cheddar cheese, shredded,
   at room temperature
1 cup (2 sticks) butter, at room temperature
2 cups chopped pecans or Rice Krispies
Chili powder, Parmesan cheese or chutney sauce
   (all optional)

1. Preheat the oven to 325 degrees.
2. Mix the garlic salt, cayenne pepper and flour in a bowl. Set aside.
3. Mix the cheese and butter in a bowl, using an electric mixer at high speed.
4. Blend the flour mixture into the cheese mixture. Fold in the chopped pecans.
5. Divide the dough into 4 equal portions. Shape and roll into 1-inch diameter cylinders. Wrap in plastic wrap and chill. Can freeze at this point (optional).
6. Cut the cylinders into slices. Place on a nonstick cookie sheet
7. Bake at 325 degrees for 15 minutes or until light brown.
8. Cool the cookies on the cookie sheet for 5 minutes. Remove to a wire rack to cool completely.
9. While the cookies are still warm, sprinkle or brush with chili powder, Parmesan cheese or chutney.

Prep Time: 20 minutes   Cook Time: 15 minutes per batch

Yield: 50 to 60 cookies

Curry powder is a combination of the following ground ingredients: coriander, turmeric, cumin, fenugreek, ginger, celery, black pepper, cinnamon, nutmeg, clove, caraway, fennel, cardamom, and salt! A variety of curry powders can be found in specialty markets and may range from the dynamite hot curries of Madras to the milder ones from Indonesia. Experiment to see which you prefer.

Curry Soup

Satisfying and spicy, smooth and rich, everyone will love this soup.

1 1/2 cups chopped cored peeled apples
1 cup chopped carrots
1 cup chopped onion
1 garlic clove, minced
1/4 cup (1/2 stick) butter
3 tablespoons all-purpose flour
1 to 2 teaspoons curry powder
1 can (16 ounces) diced tomatoes
2 to 3 cups chicken broth
1 1/2 cups cream, half-and-half, 2% milk or whole milk

1. Sauté the apples, carrots, onion and garlic in the butter in a stockpot until tender.
2. Stir in the flour and curry powder. Mix in the tomatoes and chicken broth. Cover and simmer for 40 to 45 minutes.
3. Purée the mixture in a blender or food processor.
4. Return the soup to the stockpot. Add the cream gently and reheat the mixture, stirring frequently.

Prep Time: 25 minutes   Cook Time: 40 to 45 minutes   Yield: 6 servings

French Onion Soup

A rich, delicious version of this classic soup.

2 thick slices French baguette (large enough
   to fit the top of an oven-safe soup bowl)
Butter, softened
2 tablespoons vegetable oil
1 white or yellow onion, cut into very thin strips
1 red onion, cut into very thin strips
1 garlic clove, minced
1 teaspoon chopped fresh thyme
1 bunch green onions, cut into 1- to 2-inch pieces
Salt and white pepper to taste
$1/2$ cup dry sherry
1 can (14 ounces) beef broth
1 can (14 ounces) chicken broth
3 tablespoons cornstarch
2 tablespoons butter, softened
2 cups (8 ounces) shredded Gruyère cheese

1. Preheat the oven to 350 degrees.
2. Butter the baguette slices on both sides. Bake on a baking sheet for 5 to 7 minutes. Set aside.
3. Heat the oil in a large heavy saucepan over medium heat. Sauté the white and red onions for about 20 minutes or until caramelized, stirring occasionally.
4. Add the garlic, thyme, green onions, salt and white pepper and cook for 2 minutes.
5. Add the sherry to the saucepan and cook until almost dry, stirring occasionally. Add the broths and bring to a boil.
6. Combine the cornstarch and 2 tablespoons butter in a small bowl, stirring to mix well. Add to the soup and stir until the butter mixture is melted and the soup is thickened slightly. Remove from the heat.
7. Ladle into soup bowls and cover with baguettes and cheese. Place the bowls on a baking sheet and bake for about 10 minutes or until the cheese is golden brown and bubbly.

Prep Time: 1 hour   Cook Time: 10 minutes   Yield: 2 to 3 servings

Chicken Tortilla Soup

CHEF CLYDE NELSON

1 large yellow or white onion, quartered
8 to 12 whole plum tomatoes
4 tablespoons olive oil or corn oil, divided
1 corn tortilla, chopped
4 garlic cloves, minced
1 ancho chile, stemmed, seeded,
    toasted and finely chopped
1 bay leaf
2 teaspoons toasted ground cumin seeds
8 cups chicken stock
8 ounces tomato sauce (optional)
Salt and coarsely ground pepper to taste
2 cooked chicken breasts, cut into small pieces
1 cup (4 ounces) shredded Monterey Jack cheese
1 medium avocado, peeled and diced
2 cups fried corn tortilla strips
Chopped cilantro to taste

1. Preheat the grill.
2. Rub the onion and tomatoes with 2 tablespoons of the olive oil and grill on all sides until charred or broil in the oven. Place the mixture in a blender or food processor and blend until fairly smooth. Set aside.
3. Heat the remaining 2 tablespoons olive oil in a stockpot. Add the tortilla pieces, garlic and chile. Sauté for 3 to 4 minutes.
4. Add the bay leaf, cumin and chicken stock and heat to a simmer. Stir in the blended tomato mixture and tomato sauce and simmer for 30 minutes. Add salt and pepper. Strain or leave chunky.
5. Warm the chicken and divide among 4 soup bowls. Ladle hot soup over the chicken. Garnish each serving with cheese, avocado, tortilla strips and cilantro.

Prep Time: 30 minutes   Cook Time: 30 minutes   Yield: 4 servings

Chicken Chili

Chili is a favorite wintertime meal in Steamboat, and here is a nice change from the norm, using chicken and white beans. Black or pinto beans can be substituted for a Southwestern flair.

2^1/$_2$ to 3 pounds chicken breasts
   (with skin and bones)
6 cups (or more) chicken broth
2 tablespoons extra-virgin olive oil
2 onions, chopped
8 large garlic cloves, chopped or crushed
3 or 4 fresh serrano chiles, finely chopped
   (including seeds)
1 tablespoon cumin
1 tablespoon oregano
^{1}/$_2$ teaspoon cinnamon
2 cans (15 ounces each) white beans, drained
3 to 4 cups (12 to 16 ounces) shredded
   Monterey Jack cheese
Sour cream
Tomato salsa
Lime wedges

1. Combine the chicken with the chicken broth in a 5- or 6-quart stockpot. Gently simmer the chicken for about 30 minutes or until cooked through. Skim off the fat as the chicken simmers.
2. Remove the chicken from the broth and set aside until cool. Remove and discard the skin and bones. Shred or cut into cubes. Cover with plastic wrap until ready to use.
3. Strain the broth into a large bowl.
4. Clean the stockpot. Add the olive oil and onions and sauté for about 10 minutes or until beginning to brown. Add the garlic and sauté for about 30 seconds.
5. Stir in the chiles, cumin, oregano, cinnamon, beans and broth. Partially cover the pot and simmer for about 30 minutes.
6. Stir in the chicken and simmer gently for 5 minutes or until the chicken is warmed through.
7. Stir in 1 cup of the shredded cheese just before serving.
8. Serve with side dishes of the remaining cheese, sour cream, salsa and lime wedges.

Prep Time: 30 minutes   Cook Time: 1 hour 15 minutes   Yield: 6 servings

Fresh herbs should be used whenever possible as they truly impart the best flavor! If you grow your own and have an abundance, consider drying them. Place cut herbs between two paper towels or napkins. Let them dry until they can be crumbled, and store in labeled plastic bags. Since dried herbs have a more concentrated flavor than fresh herbs, use only 1 teaspoon of dried for each tablespoon of fresh that the recipe calls for. If you are using fresh herbs in a dish that has been cooking for a long time, add some extra just before serving to liven up the flavor.

Cioppino

Put a log on the fire and enjoy this savory meal-in-a-bowl.

½ cup olive oil
2 yellow onions, finely chopped
2 red bell peppers, chopped
8 to 10 garlic cloves, crushed
1 can (28 ounces) peeled whole tomatoes
1 can (28 ounces) diced tomatoes
1 can (16 ounces) whole plum tomatoes or diced tomatoes with basil
1 tablespoon crushed red pepper
1 can (6 ounces) tomato paste
3 cans (6½ ounces each) chopped clams with juice
1 can (10 ounces) whole baby clams with juice
4 cups dry red wine, such as cabernet
3 tablespoons minced fresh basil

1 tablespoon minced fresh oregano
1 teaspoon minced fresh thyme
1 tablespoon minced fresh parsley
1 tablespoon salt
1 bottle (12 ounces) clam juice
1 tablespoon red devil cayenne pepper (or equivalent)
¼ cup (½ stick) salted butter
1½ pounds sea scallops, cut into bite-size pieces
2 pounds firm fresh fish (halibut or cod), cut into bite-size pieces
1 can crabmeat
2 pounds peeled raw medium shrimp
1 pound crab legs (optional)

1. Heat the olive oil in a large stockpot over low heat. Sauté the onions, bell peppers and garlic in the hot oil until soft.
2. Purée the whole tomatoes in a blender. Do not drain. Pour the puréed tomatoes and diced tomatoes into the stockpot.
3. Add the red pepper, tomato paste, clams, wine, basil, oregano, thyme, parsley, salt, clam juice, cayenne pepper and butter. Bring to a boil, stirring frequently. Reduce the heat and simmer, covered, for 2 hours, stirring frequently.
4. Return to a boil. Add the scallops, fish and crabmeat. Reduce the heat to low and simmer for 4 minutes. Add the shrimp and crab legs and simmer for 3 minutes.
5. Serve immediately.

Prep Time: 60 minutes   Cook Time: 2 hours 15 minutes   Yield: 12 to 15 servings

Crab Soup

A simple to make first-course soup.

6 tablespoons butter, divided
3 cups fresh mushrooms (about 9 ounces), sliced
4 tablespoons flour
4 cups chicken broth
1 cup heavy cream or fat-free half-and-half
¼ cup dry sherry
2 cups crabmeat, cooked or 3 cans (6 ounces each)

1. Heat 3 tablespoons of the butter in a skillet over medium heat.
    Add the mushrooms and sauté until tender. Remove from the heat.
2. Heat 3 tablespoons of the butter in a stockpot. Stir in the flour until blended. Add
    the chicken broth and simmer until the mixture is thickened, stirring constantly.
3. Add the cream and sherry gradually, stirring constantly. Stir in the mushrooms
    and crabmeat. Cook until heated through.
4. Serve warm.

Prep Time: 15 minutes   Cook Time: 15 minutes   Yield: 4 servings

Snow reigns supreme in Steamboat, and everyone finds a way to enjoy the tranquil beauty. The quality of the snow is so special here—deep, dry, light, and fluffy—that a local rancher dubbed it "Champagne Powder®." It takes a certain type of person to live here with the annual snowfall ranging from 170 to 450 inches, and the schools close only when the temperature is below 40 below! Braving the cold with your friends at Winter Carnival, sharing in the pride during an Olympian send-off or welcome-home, enjoying the recreational activities, coming together in a time of community need. . . these things connect us in this authentic western town.

Pomegranate Salad

Winter is the season for pomegranates, and this is a bright and beautiful salad for the holidays.

12 cups fresh spinach, washed and torn
2 avocados, peeled and sliced

3 pomegranates, seeded
Red Wine Vinaigrette (see recipe below)

1. Place the spinach greens on a large platter.
2. Arrange the avocado slices around the edge of the greens.
3. Place the pomegranate seeds in the center so that the salad resembles a wreath.
4. Serve the salad dressing on the side.

♪ To peel a pomegranate, cut the crown off the fruit. Lightly score the rind in several places. Submerge in a large bowl of cold water in the sink. Break the sections apart, separating the seeds from the membrane. The seeds will drop to the bottom of the bowl. Skim off and discard the membranes and rind. Drain the seeds into a colander; remove to paper towels to dry.

Prep Time: 20 minutes   Yield: 6 to 8 servings

Macadamia Nut & Ginger Salad

Crystallized ginger highlights this light and refreshing salad.

RED WINE VINAIGRETTE
3 tablespoons red wine vinegar
2¹/₂ teaspoons sugar
¹/₂ teaspoon salt
3 tablespoons olive oil

¹/₂ cup macadamia nuts, coarsely chopped
¹/₂ cup crystallized ginger slices, coarsely chopped
4 ounces creamy blue or Gorgonzola cheese, crumbled (optional)

SALAD
8 cups mixed greens (about one 10-ounce package)

FOR THE VINAIGRETTE:
Combine the vinegar, sugar and salt in a bowl. Whisk in the olive oil until combined.

FOR THE SALAD:
1. Toss the greens, nuts, ginger and vinaigrette in a bowl.
2. Divide the salad evenly among the plates. Arrange the cheese on top.

Prep time: 15 minutes   Yield: 4 to 6 servings

Salad of Mixed Greens, Oranges, & Pine Nuts

The peppery flavor of arugula combined with fennel and oranges gives this fun and festive salad a distinctive taste.

CHEF CLYDE NELSON

1 large bunch arugula, stemmed, washed and dried,
  or 1 package baby arugula
1 head radicchio, trimmed, washed and dried
1 large fennel bulb, trimmed, cut crosswise very thinly
3 blood oranges or navel oranges
1 to 2 teaspoons red wine vinegar
3 tablespoons extra-virgin olive oil
$1/4$ teaspoon salt
Freshly ground pepper to taste
$1/4$ cup golden raisins
$1/4$ cup pine nuts
1 teaspoon olive oil

1. Mix the salad greens and fennel in a salad bowl; chill in the refrigerator.
2. Grate $1/2$ teaspoon orange zest. Section the oranges, place in a bowl and set aside.
3. Squeeze 4 tablespoons orange juice from the leftover orange core into a bowl. Add the orange zest, vinegar, olive oil, salt and pepper and whisk together. Add the raisins and marinate for 10 minutes. Remove and set aside.
4. Sauté the pine nuts in the olive oil in a skillet until golden brown.
5. Toss the salad greens with the vinaigrette. Place on individual serving plates and garnish with orange sections, pine nuts and raisins. Serve at once.

Prep Time: 30 minute   Yield: 10 to 12 small servings

The magic of summer continues into the holiday season as Strings presents the youth concert Moguls to Mozart. The audience, often still in ski attire, comes from the hill and into the Steamboat Sheraton Resort, where the concert is held. Hundreds of children and their families gather to delight in the performance followed by cookies and lemonade. One of these concerts, "Mozart's Magical Life and Music," became the basis of the Festival's award-winning children's interactive Web site, appropriately named "Moguls to Mozart."

Spinach Salad with Avocado, Oranges, & Feta

With the irresistible tangy-sweet vinaigrette, this salad will quickly become a favorite.

^{1}/3 cup rice vinegar
3 tablespoons sugar
1 teaspoon salt
^{1}/2 teaspoon toasted sesame oil
^{1}/2 teaspoon ground black pepper
^{1}/2 cup vegetable oil (canola or olive)
Spinach leaves, washed and dried (6 ounces)
1 head romaine, washed, dried and torn
^{1}/2 cup dried cranberries
^{1}/2 cup pecans, toasted and chopped
4 to 8 ounces feta or blue cheese, drained and crumbled
1 or 2 ripe avocados, peeled and cubed
1 can mandarin orange slices, drained
^{1}/2 red onion, sliced

1. Mix the vinegar, sugar, salt, sesame oil, pepper and oil in a small bowl.
2. Toss the spinach and romaine together in a salad bowl. Top the greens with the cranberries, pecans, cheese, avocados, mandarin oranges and red onion.
3. Drizzle about half the vinaigrette over the salad and toss to coat thoroughly. Drizzle with additional dressing if needed.

Prep Time: 25 minutes   Yield: 8 servings

Asian Chicken Salad

Freshies is a family-style restaurant located between the town and the mountain.

CHEF GREG MARGOLIS

8 boneless skinless chicken breasts (5 ounces each),
  pounded to even thickness
1 cup sweet soy sauce
  (available at specialty food stores)
1 large carrot, peeled and shredded
3 ribs celery, cut into small strips
1 red bell pepper, cut into small strips
$^1/_3$ bunch cilantro, roughly chopped
$^1/_2$ cup toasted sesame oil
$^1/_2$ cup soy sauce
$^1/_2$ cup mirin
1 ($^1/_2$-inch) piece fresh ginger, peeled and grated
Chopped lettuce
Udon noodles, cooked
Chopped fresh cilantro (optional)
Pickled ginger (optional)

1. Marinate the chicken in the sweet soy sauce in a sealable plastic bag in the refrigerator for 2 hours.
2. Mix together the carrot, celery, bell pepper and cilantro.
3. Preheat the grill. Drain the chicken, discarding the marinade. Place the chicken on a grill rack and grill for 10 to 15 minutes or until the chicken is cooked through. Cool and cut into thin strips. Combine with the vegetables in bowl.
4. Combine the sesame oil, soy sauce, mirin and grated ginger in a bowl. Pour over the chicken mixture and toss to coat.
5. Serve on a bed of chopped lettuce and udon noodles. Garnish with chopped fresh cilantro and pickled ginger.

Prep Time: 15 to 20 minutes   Marinate Time: 2 hours

Cook Time: 10 to 15 minutes   Yield: 8 to 10 servings

Beef Tenderloin with Mushroom & Wine Sauce

Even if you prefer beef tenderloin unadorned, give this recipe a try as the sauce is really delicious and simple to prepare. It can be assembled in the morning and chilled. Bring to room temperature before baking.

1/4 cup (1/2 stick) butter
2 garlic cloves, crushed
16 ounces fresh mushrooms, sliced
2 large onions, peeled and sliced
8 slices bacon, chopped
1/4 cup bottled chili sauce
1/2 teaspoon marjoram
1/2 teaspoon thyme
8 drops of Tabasco sauce

4 dashes of Worcestershire sauce
1 1/4 cups dry red wine
4 beef bouillon cubes
Salt and pepper to taste
2 tablespoons all-purpose flour
1 whole beef tenderloin (4 to 5 pounds), trimmed and tied

1. Preheat the oven to 450 degrees.
2. Melt the butter in a large skillet. Add the garlic, mushrooms, onions and bacon and sauté for 5 to 10 minutes, stirring occasionally.
3. Add the chili sauce, marjoram, thyme, Tabasco sauce, Worcestershire sauce, wine and bouillon cubes. Season with salt and pepper. Sprinkle with the flour and stir to combine. Simmer for 20 minutes.
4. Place the tenderloin in a large roasting pan. Pour the onion mixture over the tenderloin and cover with foil.
5. Bake for 35 to 40 minutes, checking the temperature with an instant-read thermometer after 25 minutes. The internal temperature should reach 130 to 135 degrees. Remove from the oven. Keep warm and let stand for 15 minutes.
6. Slice the tenderloin and serve the sauce on the side.

 Sea level may need less cooking time.

Prep Time: 40 minutes   Cook Time: 35 to 40 minutes

Yield: 10 to 12 servings

Esterhazy Steak

Hungarian comfort food. This goes well with mashed potatoes.

2 pounds round steak ($1/2$- to $3/4$-inch thick)
$1/2$ cup plus 1 tablespoon flour, divided
2 teaspoons salt
$1/2$ teaspoon pepper
$1/4$ cup plus 1 tablespoon canola oil, divided
3 carrots, peeled and thinly sliced

2 small onions, thinly sliced
1 parsnip, thinly sliced
1 rib celery, chopped
1 to 2 teaspoons capers, drained
1 cup beef broth
$1/4$ cup white wine
1 cup sour cream
1 teaspoon sweet paprika (Hungarian paprika)

1. Preheat the oven to 350 degrees. Grease a 7x11-inch baking dish.
2. Place the steak on a cutting board. Mix $1/2$ cup flour, salt and pepper in a small bowl. Sprinkle $1/2$ of the mixture over the steak and pound in with a meat mallet, a saucer edge or a rolling pin. Turn the steak over and repeat the process with the remaining flour mixture.
3. Heat $1/4$ cup canola oil in a large skillet. Slowly brown the steak on both sides in the hot oil. Remove to the baking dish.
4. Add the carrots, onions, parsnip and celery to the skillet and cook over medium heat for 10 minutes, stirring occasionally. If the oil in the pan is too brown, discard and add 2 tablespoons fresh oil. Add the capers. Spoon the vegetables over and around the steak.
5. Heat the remaining 1 tablespoon canola oil in a small saucepan. Blend in the remaining 1 tablespoon flour. Heat until the mixture bubbles and browns lightly, stirring constantly. Slowly add the beef broth, stirring constantly. Rapidly bring to a boil. Remove from the heat and stir in the wine. If necessary, add a small amount of the beef broth, but the sauce should not be too thin.
6. Pour the sauce over the vegetables and cover the baking dish tightly with foil.
7. Bake for $1 1/4$ hours or until the steak is tender.
8. Remove from the oven and let cool for several minutes. Slowly blend the sour cream and paprika into the sauce. If the sauce is too hot, the sour cream will begin to curdle. Just stop and let it cool for several minutes longer.
9. Return to the oven. Bake, uncovered, for about 15 minutes longer or until the steak is fork-tender.

Prep Time 30 minutes   Cook Time $1 1/2$ hours   Yield: 6 servings

Beef Stew with Garlic Mashed Potatoes

A classy variation on a winter comfort food.

STEW

2 pounds New York strip,
   sirloin or tenderloin steak

1/2 cup all-purpose flour

6 tablespoons extra-virgin
   olive oil, divided

3 sprigs of fresh thyme

1/4 cup finely chopped onion

2 garlic cloves, finely chopped

2 cups vegetable stock

1 cup plus 3 tablespoons
   water

3/4 teaspoon grated orange
   zest

1 teaspoon kosher salt

1/2 teaspoon ground pepper

1/2 teaspoon sugar

1 cup zinfandel or burgundy

1 pound baby carrots

1 cup chopped onion

1 cup fresh or frozen peas

8 ounces fresh mushrooms,
   quartered

1 teaspoon cornstarch

2 tablespoons chopped fresh
   flat-leaf parsley for garnish

MASHED POTATOES

4 pounds white or gold
   potatoes, peeled and
   chopped

4 garlic cloves

1 1/2 teaspoons kosher salt

1/4 cup (1/2 stick) butter

1/2 cup sour cream

1/2 cup (about) cream or milk

FOR THE STEW:

1. Cut the steak into 1-inch cubes and remove excess fat. Roll in the flour to coat.
2. Heat 4 tablespoons olive oil in an 8-quart stockpot over medium heat. Add 2 sprigs of thyme and cook until the oil starts to smoke. Discard the thyme.
3. Add the beef to the stockpot and cook for about 5 minutes or until brown on all sides and juices just begin to run. Remove and set aside.
4. Add the remaining 2 tablespoons olive oil and 1/4 cup onion to the stockpot. Cook for about 3 minutes or just until the onion starts to brown. Add the garlic.
5. Return the beef to the stockpot. Add the remaining sprig of thyme, vegetable stock, 1 cup water, orange zest, salt, pepper, sugar and wine. Boil gently for 15 minutes to slightly reduce the liquid. Add the carrots and 1 cup onion. Reduce the heat. Simmer, covered, for 30 minutes. Add the peas and mushrooms.
6. Stir together the remaining 3 tablespoons water and cornstarch until smooth. Add slowly to the stew. Simmer, uncovered, for 5 minutes to thicken.

FOR THE MASHED POTATOES:

1. Place the potatoes and garlic in a large saucepan of boiling water. Add the salt and simmer for 20 minutes or until the potatoes are very tender.
2. Drain the potatoes and garlic. Return to the pan. Add the butter, sour cream and a little cream or milk. Mash coarsely, adding additional cream as necessary for the desired consistency. Season with salt to taste. Serve in large shallow bowls with stew atop potatoes and garnished with parsley.

Prep Time: 40 minutes   Cook Time: 1 hour 15 minutes   Yield: 8 servings

Peppered Elk Steaks with Port Glaze

The flavors of each peppercorn, the garlic, and the hearty wine glaze complement the rich flavor of the elk perfectly in this very peppery meat dish. Four-pepper blend may be substituted if your pantry does not include this variety of peppercorn.

CHEF DAVID NELSON

2 elk loin steaks (7 ounces each) or
    venison loin steaks or beef sirloin
2 tablespoons olive oil
1 teaspoon chopped garlic
$1/2$ teaspoon crushed black peppercorns
$1/2$ teaspoon crushed red peppercorns
$1/2$ teaspoon crushed green peppercorns
$1/2$ teaspoon crushed white peppercorns
Salt to taste
Balsamic Port Glaze (see recipe below)

1. If the steaks are frozen, thaw in the refrigerator overnight. Prior to cooking, remove the steaks from the refrigerator and allow to come to room temperature.
2. Mix the olive oil, garlic, peppercorns and salt in a small bowl. Rub on the steaks and marinate for about 30 minutes, turning occasionally.
3. Preheat the grill to medium-hot.
4. Grill the steaks for about 12 minutes for medium-rare or to desired doneness.
5. Serve the steaks over a pool of balsamic port glaze on warmed dinner plates.

Prep Time: 10 minutes   Cook Time: 12 minutes   Marinate Time: 30 minutes

Yield: 2 servings

Balsamic Port Glaze

$1/2$ cup port
$1/2$ cup balsamic vinegar
$1/2$ teaspoon minced garlic
$1/8$ teaspoon cracked pepper

Combine the port, vinegar, garlic, and cracked pepper in a saucepan and bring to a boil. Cook at a low boil until reduced by half, about 10 to 12 minutes.

Mediterranean Lamb Shanks with Polenta

Café Diva prepares a new menu each season, focusing on the freshest market ingredients. It's located in the heart of the Mountain Village.

Enjoy the tender and luscious qualities of lamb.

CHEF KATE VAN RENSSELAER

6 medium lamb shanks
   (about 4¹/₂ pounds total)
Salt and pepper to taste
3 tablespoons olive oil,
   divided
1 large onion, cut into
   ¹/₂-inch pieces
3 large carrots, cut into
   ¹/₂-inch pieces
4 ribs celery, cut into
   ¹/₂-inch pieces
6 large garlic cloves, chopped
3 large fresh rosemary sprigs

3 large fresh thyme sprigs
1 can (28 ounces) diced
   tomatoes in juice
2¹/₄ cups low-sodium
   chicken broth
1 tablespoon whole black
   peppercorns
8 cups water
2 teaspoons salt
2 cups polenta or
   yellow cornmeal
¹/₄ cup (¹/₂ stick) butter
2 teaspoons minced thyme

1. Preheat the oven to 350 degrees. Sprinkle the lamb with salt and pepper.
2. Heat 2 tablespoons olive oil in a large ovenproof stockpot over high heat. Add the lamb and brown on all sides. Using tongs, remove the lamb to a plate.
3. Add the remaining 1 tablespoon olive oil to the stockpot. Add the onion, carrots, celery and garlic. Sauté for about 10 minutes or until the vegetables brown and begin to soften, scraping up any browned bits.
4. Return the lamb to the stockpot, pushing gently into the vegetables. Add the rosemary sprigs, thyme sprigs, tomatoes, chicken broth and peppercorns. Bring to a boil over high heat. Cover the stockpot; remove to the oven. Bake for about 2 hours or until the lamb is tender and pulls easily from the bone, turning occasionally.
5. Bring the water and salt to a boil in a large saucepan over high heat. Gradually whisk in the polenta. Reduce the heat to medium-low and simmer for about 22 minutes or until thickened and tender, stirring frequently. Whisk in the butter and minced thyme. Season with salt and pepper.
6. Remove the lamb and herbs from the stockpot. Discard the herbs. Place the stockpot over medium-high heat and boil for about 5 minutes or until the sauce is slightly thickened.
7. Divide the polenta evenly among 6 large bowls; top each with 1 lamb shank. Ladle the sauce over the lamb and serve.

Prep Time: 35 minutes   Cook Time: 2 hours   Yield: 6 servings

Lamb Stroganoff in Puff Pastry Crust

CHEF JACQUES WILSON

2¹/₂ pounds lamb shoulder,
 or 2 pounds top round,
 well trimmed and cut into
 small cubes
Salt and pepper to taste
2 tablespoons vegetable oil
2 tablespoons butter
¹/₄ cup minced shallots
1 pound assorted wild
 mushrooms, sliced (such
 as crimini, chanterelle,
 portobello and shiitake)
2 ounces (1 large bulb)
 roasted garlic cloves
 peeled and left whole

¹/₂ cup all-purpose flour
1 cup beef broth
¹/₂ cup red wine
1 sheet puff pastry
 (12x12-inch), cut to fit
 tops of baking dishes
³/₄ cup crème fraîche or
 heavy cream
1 tablespoon Dijon mustard
1 tablespoon chopped fresh
 herbs (parsley, thyme and
 a little rosemary)
Egg wash (1 egg beaten with
 1 teaspoon water)

Jacques Wilson, CEC, AAC,
is an award-winning chef
recently inducted into the
American Academy of Chefs,
the honor society of the
American Culinary
Federation. He is currently
the Executive Chef/Director
of Food Service at the
Yampa Valley Medical
Center. Chef Jacques teaches
virtually any food-related
subject, including teaching
youngsters at primary
schools about the importance
of nutrition.

1. Preheat the oven to 350 degrees. Coat 4 (8 to 10 ounces each) individual baking dishes or a 2¹/₂-quart baking dish with nonstick cooking spray.

2. Pat the lamb dry with paper towels. Sprinkle with salt and pepper. Heat the oil in a heavy 12-inch skillet over high heat until very hot. Reduce the heat to medium and, working in batches, add the lamb in a single layer and cook just until brown on the outside, about 1 minute per side. Remove the lamb from the pan.

3. Melt the butter in the same skillet over medium-high heat. Add the lamb and shallots and cook for about 2 minutes or until the shallots are tender. Add the mushrooms and garlic. Sprinkle with pepper and sauté for about 5 minutes. Blend in the flour, stirring to thicken. Add the beef broth and wine. Simmer for about 30 minutes or until the liquid thickens and just coats the mushrooms.

4. Thaw the puff pastry and cut to fit the baking dishes (a paper pattern helps).

5. Add the crème fraîche, mustard and herbs to the lamb mixture and stir to combine. Remove to the baking dishes.

6. Place the puff pastry on top of the stroganoff in the dishes. Make 2 slits in the top of each pastry and brush with egg wash. Bake for 15 to 20 minutes or until the tops are golden brown.

♪ To roast garlic, break the bulb in half, place on foil, drizzle with 1 teaspoon olive oil and season with salt to taste. Bake in a 350-degree oven for 1 hour. Remove the garlic from its skin by squeezing with thumb and forefinger. This step can be done 2 days ahead, when the oven is already in use. Store in the refrigerator until needed.

Prep Time: 50 minutes   Cook Time: 60 minutes   Yield: 4 servings

Roast Pork with Cream Sauce

Simple and elegant, this much-loved recipe comes directly from Rome.

Everyone has a favorite place to follow up a fine day on the slopes or trails, nurturing the soul in the company of good friends with good food. Visitors and locals alike cozy up to get warm in homes and restaurants around town, describing the day's adventures. Savoring the food and enjoying refreshments while connecting with longtime friends and making new ones is about as good as it gets.

1 (3-pound) boneless pork roast
1 garlic clove, mashed
$^1/_2$ to 1 teaspoon sage
Salt and freshly ground pepper to taste
$^1/_4$ cup coarsely chopped onion
$^1/_4$ cup coarsely chopped carrots
2 cups heavy cream

1. Preheat the oven to 350 degrees.
2. Rub the pork all over with the garlic, sage, salt and pepper. Place on a rack in a small roasting pan.
3. Bake for 1$^1/_2$ hours. About halfway through the cooking time, spread the onion and carrots around the roast and continue baking.
4. Remove from the oven and take the rack out of the pan. Pour off most of the accumulated pan juices and place the pork directly on the bottom of the pan. Pour the cream over the pork and vegetables.
5. Return to the oven and bake for 15 minutes longer, basting the pork 1 or 2 times with the cream. The cream should thicken and mix with the pan juices to become a wonderful sauce.
6. Test the pork with a meat thermometer; it should register about 145 degrees. The pork should be slightly pink inside and still juicy.
7. Remove the pork to a serving plate and let stand for about 10 minutes. Slice the pork.
8. If the sauce is too thin, boil for a few minutes to reduce slightly and thicken. Strain the sauce and discard the vegetables. Serve the sauce on the side.

Serving Suggestion: Good served with a bulgur wheat pilaf or mushroom orzo.

Prep Time: 5 minutes   Cook Time: 1 hour 45 minutes   Yield: 6 to 8 servings

Pizza Roll

This calzone variation is filled with healthy vegetables, meat, and cheese.

DOUGH
1 package active dry yeast
1 cup warm water
1 tablespoon sugar
1 teaspoon salt
$2^1/_2$ to 3 cups all-purpose
  flour

FILLING
8 ounces ham or Italian
  sausages, casings removed
1 tablespoon olive oil
8 ounces mushrooms, sliced
$^1/_2$ onion, sliced
$^1/_2$ green bell pepper,
  chopped

1 garlic clove, minced
1 package (10 ounces) frozen
  chopped spinach, thawed,
  excess water removed
$2^1/_2$ cups (10 ounces)
  shredded mozzarella
  cheese
1 tablespoon Italian
  seasoning
Salt and pepper to taste

ASSEMBLY
Olive oil
$^1/_3$ cup grated
  Parmesan cheese
Freshly ground pepper

FOR THE DOUGH:
1. Dissolve the yeast in the water in a large bowl. Let stand for about 5 minutes. Add the sugar, salt, and $1^1/_2$ cups flour and beat until smooth. Stir in the remaining flour to make the dough easy to handle.
2. Turn the dough onto a lightly floured surface and knead for 3 minutes. Shape into a ball and place in an oiled bowl. Let rise, covered, in a warm place for 1 hour.

FOR THE FILLING:
1. Cut the ham into bite-size pieces and cook using the package directions in a large skillet or brown the sausage over medium heat for 5 to 8 minutes or until crumbly.
2. Heat the oil in a skillet over medium heat. Add the mushrooms, onion, bell pepper and garlic and sauté until soft and light brown.
3. Combine the vegetable mixture, meat, spinach, mozzarella cheese, Italian seasoning, salt and pepper in a large bowl and mix well.

TO ASSEMBLE:
1. Preheat the oven to 375 degrees. Lightly oil a jellyroll pan.
2. Roll the dough into a 12x15-inch rectangle on a lightly floured board. Spread the filling over the dough, leaving a 1-inch strip on the long side. Roll tightly and place seam side down on the prepared pan. Brush the roll with oil and sprinkle with Parmesan cheese and pepper. Pierce the top with a fork in several places.
3. Bake for about 40 minutes or until golden brown. Let stand for 10 minutes.

Prep Time: 40 minutes   Rise Time: 1 hour   Cook Time: 40 minutes

Yield: 4 servings

Cassoulet

A simplified version of the classic French dish, which is great for cold winter nights. Easy to prepare in separate stages.

1 pound dried Great Northern beans
12 thick slices bacon, cut into 1-inch pieces
3 large onions, sliced
1 can (28 ounces) chopped tomatoes, including juice
Freshly ground pepper to taste
4 garlic cloves, minced
$1/2$ teaspoon thyme
5 sprigs of parsley, chopped
1 large bay leaf
3 cups chicken stock (can used canned)
1 pound pork shoulder, trimmed and cubed
1 pound lamb shoulder, trimmed and cubed
   (can use lamb shoulder chops)
1 pound Polish sausage, cut into $1/2$-inch slices
   (can use Italian sausage)
Olive oil

1. Soak the beans using the package directions (either overnight or quick-soak).
2. Cook the beans in boiling water in a heavy saucepan for $1^1/2$ to 2 hours or until almost done; drain.
3. Cook the bacon in a sauté pan, until it just begins to render some fat. Add the onions and sauté for at least 20 minutes or until the bacon begins to brown and the onions almost disappear, stirring frequently; drain well.
4. Slowly add the undrained tomatoes, scraping up any browned bits from the bottom of the pan. Stir in the pepper, garlic, thyme, parsley, bay leaf and chicken stock. Simmer for 15 minutes.
5. Brown the pork, lamb and sausage in olive oil in small batches in a skillet.
6. Preheat the oven to 325 degrees
7. Place enough beans to cover the bottom in a Dutch oven. Top with the pork, lamb, sausage, remaining beans and onion mixture. Stir gently to combine.
8. Cover and bake for 1 to $1^1/2$ hours, skimming fat if necessary. Remove the bay leaf before serving.
9. May refrigerate up to 2 days before serving or freezing. Reheat slowly.

Prep Time: $1^1/2$ hours   Soak Time: Overnight

Cook Time: $2^1/2$ to $3^1/2$ hours   Yield: 8 to 12 servings

Chicken & Fennel in Red Wine Sauce

Be adventuresome and try fresh fennel, which imparts an unusual flavor to chicken.

8 chicken thighs
Salt and pepper to taste
1 tablespoon olive oil
1 sweet onion, peeled, quartered and thinly sliced
4 garlic cloves, chopped
2 fennel bulbs, cut into $^1/_8$-inch slices
1 teaspoon dried herbs, such as thyme or
  herbes de Provence
2 cups red wine
Chicken stock
$^1/_2$ cup pitted kalamata olives, cut into halves

1. Season the chicken with salt and pepper. Heat the olive oil in a deep skillet over medium-high heat and sear the chicken on both sides in the hot oil. Remove to a plate.
2. Reduce the heat to medium. Sauté the onion and garlic in the skillet until soft and translucent. Add the chicken, fennel, herbs, wine and enough chicken stock to cover the chicken, about 1 to 2 cups. Bring to a simmer and reduce the heat to low. Cover and cook for 30 minutes.
3. Remove the chicken to a platter or shallow serving bowl and keep warm. Increase the heat to medium-high and add the olives to the skillet. Cook until the sauce is reduced and thickened and the fennel is soft. If needed, thicken the sauce with a tablespoon of flour mixed with a little chicken stock.
4. Serve on dinner plates or in shallow bowls.

Serving Suggestion: Hot French bread and a salad with vinaigrette dressing are great accompaniments.

♪ To prepare the fennel bulb for this dish, trim off $^1/_4$ inch from the root end, then cut off the stalks about 1 inch above the bulb. Keeping the core intact, slice $^1/_8$ inch thick.

Prep Time: 10 minutes   Cook Time: 45 to 60 minutes   Yield: 4 servings

Although fennel is relatively new to many Americans, it is actually one of the world's oldest-known edible plants. Valued by the ancient Romans for its medicinal qualities, this Tuscan vegetable is sometimes mislabeled "anise" in our produce sections. Fennel has a large bulb base and long celery-like stalks with feathery fronds. The subtle licorice flavor mellows when it is cooked, but it is equally delicious raw. Try cutting the bulb into strips and dipping in olive oil and coarse salt and pepper as an appetizer; or use in any variety of salads.

Green Chile & Chicken Alfredo

A marvelous combination of New Mexican and Italian flavors. If fresh chiles are unavailable, substitute frozen or canned.

3 whole chicken breasts
8 to 12 ounces farfalle (bow tie pasta)
1/2 cup (1 stick) butter
2 tablespoons olive oil
2 or 3 garlic cloves, minced or crushed
1 cup heavy cream or chicken stock
2 teaspoons cornstarch
1/2 cup low-fat milk
1 cup chopped roasted fresh New Mexican green chili
Salt to taste
1 to 2 cups freshly grated Parmesan cheese
1 cup walnut halves, toasted and lightly salted
   (toast in a 350-degree oven for 8 to 10 minutes,
   stirring occasionally)
Freshly ground pepper to taste

1. Broil or grill the chicken for about 10 to 12 minutes or until the juices run clear. Slice or cube the chicken. Set aside and keep warm.
2. Cook the pasta in boiling water in a stockpot using the package directions; drain.
3. Melt the butter with the olive oil in a large saucepan over medium heat. Sauté the garlic for about 3 minutes, being careful not to burn it. Slowly stir in the cream and bring the sauce just to a boil.
4. Combine the cornstarch with the milk in a bowl and blend into the sauce to thicken. Add the green chili, chicken and salt and heat through. Stir in the cooked pasta, cheese and walnuts.
5. Season with freshly ground pepper.

Prep Time: 40 minutes   Cook Time: 25 minutes   Yield: 6 to 8 servings

Chicken with Artichoke Hearts

¹/₄ cup bread crumbs

¹/₄ cup flour

1 teaspoon salt

¹/₂ teaspoon freshly ground pepper

8 chicken breasts, or a combination of
   breasts and thighs

¹/₄ cup olive oil

2 garlic cloves, minced

3 jars (6 ounces each) artichoke hearts,
   marinated in oil

2 cups sliced fresh mushrooms

1 cup dry white wine

1. Preheat the oven to 350 degrees.
2. Mix together the bread crumbs, flour, salt and pepper in a shallow bowl. Coat the chicken with the mixture.
3. Heat the olive oil in large skillet and add the garlic. Lightly brown the chicken on all sides and place in a baking dish.
4. Pour the marinated artichoke hearts and mushrooms over the browned chicken. Add the wine.
5. Bake for 40 minutes, basting frequently. Add additional wine as needed.
6. Serve warm.

Serving Suggestion: Serve with creamy polenta and a salad of sliced fresh tomatoes.

Prep Time: 30 minutes   Cook Time: 40 minutes   Yield: 8 servings

Romance is in the air, and everyone loves the delicious food served each year at Strings' Valentine's Progressive Dinner. A much-anticipated event, tickets are coveted for this special evening. Friends of Strings open their homes, and guests are transported from house to house, enjoying hors d'oeuvres, soup, entrées, and desserts. Hosts and hostesses graciously provide an intimate ambiance along with fine food and wine for this legant affair.

Chicken Parmesan

Cooper and Tracy Barnett offer the Chicken Parmesan recipe, which has been served for the past 20 years at Mazzola's Restaurant. As Mazzola's evolves under new ownership, the recipes will change, but the same family-friendly philosophy will remain.

4 chicken breasts, lightly pounded to an even thickness
$^1/_2$ cup Italian salad dressing
$^1/_2$ cup seasoned Italian bread crumbs
Olive oil
$^1/_2$ cup homemade or bottled marinara sauce
$^1/_2$ cup (2 ounces) shredded mozzarella cheese

1. Marinate the chicken in the Italian dressing in the refrigerator for at least 1 hour or overnight. Remove the chicken from the marinade, discarding the marinade.
2. Just before cooking, dredge the chicken in the bread crumbs.
3. Preheat the oven to 350 degrees.
4. Heat a small amount of olive oil in a skillet over medium heat. Add the breaded chicken. Cook until brown and partially cooked through, about 4 minutes per side.
5. Spray a shallow baking dish with nonstick cooking spray. Spread a small amount of marinara sauce over the bottom of the dish. Arrange the browned chicken on the marinara sauce. Top with additional marinara (not too much. . .it will make it soggy) and sprinkle with the cheese. Bake for 12 to 15 minutes or until the sauce is bubbly and the cheese is melted and light brown and the chicken is cooked through.

To make a sandwich, slit an 8-inch hoagie roll in half lengthwise. Lightly spread marinara sauce on both sides of the roll. Slice a fully cooked breaded chicken breast and arrange on the bottom half of the roll. Lightly top with marinara sauce and mozzarella cheese. Melt the cheese under the broiler in the oven, watching carefully to avoid burning. Place the top of the roll on the sandwich and enjoy.

Prep Time: 10 minutes   Marinate Time: 1 hour to overnight

Cook Time: 20 to 22 minutes   Yield: 4 servings

Cornish Hen & Wild Rice Supreme

*This recipe multiplies well and was served at one of the
Strings' Valentine's Progressive Dinners.*

2 Cornish game hens, thawed and split into halves
3 tablespoons butter, divided
1 package (6 ounces) long grain and wild rice mix
$^1/_2$ cup sliced green onions
6 large mushrooms, sliced
$^1/_2$ cup dry white wine
1 can (14$^1/_2$ ounces) chicken broth
2 bay leaves

1. Preheat the oven to 450 degrees.
2. Rinse the hens and pat dry. Brush inside and out with 1 tablespoon melted butter. Remove the seasoning packet from the rice. Using $^1/_2$ teaspoon per hen half, sprinkle the seasoning over the outside skin. Place the hens breast side up in a 9x13-inch baking pan. Bake for 15 minutes.
3. Melt the remaining 2 tablespoons butter in a large skillet. Add the green onions, mushrooms and rice. Sauté for about 3 to 4 minutes, stirring occasionally. Slowly add the remaining seasoning, wine, chicken broth and bay leaves. Bring to a boil.
4. Pour the rice mixture into the pan around the hens.
5. Reduce the oven temperature to 350 degrees and bake for 45 minutes longer or until all the liquid is absorbed. Discard the bay leaves.

Prep Time: 30 minutes   Cook Time: 1 hour 15 minutes   Yield: 4 servings

Teriyaki Salmon

The addition of orange sets this salmon's sauce apart from other teriyakis.

1 (1-pound) salmon, skin removed
4 or 5 garlic cloves, slivered
1 (1-inch) piece fresh gingerroot, slivered
Juice of 1 lemon
$^1/_4$ cup teriyaki marinade
2 tablespoon frozen orange juice concentrate

1. Make slits on both sides of the salmon. Insert the garlic slivers alternately with the ginger root slivers.
2. Drench both sides of the salmon with lemon juice. Place in an ungreased baking dish. Pour the teriyaki sauce over the salmon. Spoon the unthawed orange juice concentrate over the salmon.
3. Marinate the salmon in the refrigerator for 1 to 2 hours. Turn the salmon once and let marinate for an additional 1 hour.
4. Preheat the oven to 350 degrees. Remove the salmon from the refrigerator so that the salmon and baking dish can both warm up before baking. Discard the marinade.
5. Bake for 20 to 30 minutes or until the salmon flakes easily with a fork. Do not overcook.

Serving Suggestion: Serve with wild rice and a green vegetable.

Prep Time: 25 minutes   Marinate Time: 2 to 3 hours
Cook Time: 20 to 30 minutes   Yield: 4 servings

Baked Salmon in Mustard Crumb Crust

3 tablespoons white vinegar
2 tablespoons sugar
3 tablespoons Dijon mustard
$^1/_2$ teaspoon dry mustard
$^1/_2$ cup olive oil
1 (1$^1/_4$-pound) salmon fillet
$^1/_2$ teaspoon thyme
Salt and pepper
1$^1/_2$ to 1$^3/_4$ cups fresh bread crumbs

1. Preheat the oven to 375 degrees.
2. Place the vinegar, sugar and mustards in a blender. With the blender running on low, pour the olive oil in slowly until well blended.
3. Place the salmon skin side down in a foil-lined baking pan and pat dry. Season with the thyme, salt and pepper. Sprinkle the mustard mixture evenly over the salmon, making sure it is completely covered. Press the bread crumbs onto the fish.
4. Bake for 25 to 30 minutes or until the crumb crust is golden brown and the fish flakes easily with a fork.

Prep Time: 15 minutes   Cook Time: 25 to 30 minutes   Yield: 3 to 4 servings

Fresh or dry bread crumbs are often recommended for adding body and texture to stuffing or for providing a crisp topping for broiled or baked dishes. Make them yourself by choosing a good quality, rustic-style loaf of wheat bread that has a coarse-textured crumb. For fresh bread crumbs, break up the bread and process in a food processor until the desired consistency is reached. For dry bread crumbs, proceed as for fresh, but then place the crumbs on a baking sheet and bake at 250 degrees for approximately one hour, until thoroughly dried. Mix in some dried herbs, if desired.

Shrimp Creole

Here is an easy and mildly spicy entrée to serve after a day outdoors.

$^1/_4$ cup ($^1/_2$ stick) butter
1 green bell pepper, finely chopped
1 red bell pepper, finely chopped
1 onion, finely chopped
3 garlic cloves, minced
1 can (14 ounces) stewed tomatoes
1 bay leaf
$^1/_4$ teaspoon red pepper flakes or Tabasco sauce, or to taste
$^1/_2$ teaspoon salt
$^1/_4$ teaspoon freshly ground pepper
1 pound fresh shrimp, peeled and deveined, with tails on
Hot cooked rice

1. Melt the butter in a 12-inch sauté pan. Add the bell peppers, onion and garlic. Sauté for about 5 minutes or until tender.
2. Add the tomatoes, bay leaf, red pepper flakes, salt and pepper. Simmer, partially covered, for 30 minutes. Add a little water or tomato juice if necessary to maintain the sauce.
3. Add the shrimp and simmer for 5 minutes longer or until the shrimp is opaque and tender. Remove the bay leaf.
4. Serve over a bed of hot cooked rice.

Prep Time: 15 minutes   Cook Time: 40 minutes   Yield: 4 servings

Dom's Penne Portobello

Riggio's Fine Italian Food is located in downtown Steamboat Springs.
The modern upscale décor provides a unique dining experience.

CHEF DOMINICK RIGGIO

1 pound penne
¼ cup olive oil
1 or 2 portobello mushroom caps, thinly sliced
1 onion, finely chopped
2 ounces prosciutto, chopped
½ cup marsala
1 pint (2 cups) heavy cream
1½ cups frozen green peas
Salt and pepper to taste
1 cup grated Romano cheese
2 tablespoons chopped parsley

1. Cook the pasta using the package directions. Drain and set aside.
2. Heat the olive oil in a heavy saucepan. Add the mushrooms, onion and prosciutto and sauté until the onion browns slightly.
3. Add the marsala to deglaze, stirring to loosen and blend in browned bits, until the volume is reduced by half.
4. Add the heavy cream and bring to a boil.
5. Add the green peas, salt and pepper. Reduce the heat and simmer for about 3 minutes.
6. Toss the hot cooked pasta with the sauce. Add the cheese and parsley. Serve immediately.

Prep Time: 20 minutes   Cook Time: 25 minutes   Yield: 4 to 6 servings

To minimize the tearing of eyes when slicing onions, peel the onions and leave at room temperature for one hour. When the integrity of an onion's cell structure is changed by cutting, sulfuric compounds and enzymes are released, which then form another compound that irritates the eyes. As an alternative, if you cut onions near a lit candle, the flame oxidizes and eliminates most of the irritating compound.

Garlic is a vegetable and a member of the lily family, along with onions, shallots, leeks, green onions, and asparagus. Fresh garlic is always preferred to garlic salt, powder, or jarred minced garlic. To easily peel the garlic, place a clove on a cutting board, and crush it with the flat side of a chef's knife by striking the knife with your hand. This should allow you to peel it more easily. Garlic is mildest as a whole unpeeled clove and strongest minced through a press. Raw garlic is stronger than cooked.

Favorite Spaghetti Sauce

Don't be put off by the long list of ingredients as it goes together quickly and will soon live up to its name.

1/4 cup (1/2 stick) butter
1/4 cup olive oil
2 green bell peppers, chopped
2 onions, chopped
3 garlic cloves, minced
1 pound ground beef
1 pound Italian link sausage, cut into 1-inch pieces, or bulk Italian sausage
1/2 teaspoon rosemary
1 teaspoon basil
1 teaspoon oregano
2 beef bouillon cubes
1 bay leaf

1/2 teaspoon chili powder
1/2 teaspoon fennel seeds
1 can (28 ounces) tomatoes, cut up
2 cans (15 ounces each) tomato sauce
1 cup water
1 cup dry red wine
2 cans (6 ounces each) tomato paste
2 tablespoons sugar
1/4 cup chopped parsley
1/2 cup grated Parmesan cheese

1. Melt the butter with the olive oil in a 12-inch sauté pan.
2. Add the bell peppers, onions and garlic. Sauté for about 10 minutes or until soft and fragrant. Set aside.
3. Sauté the ground beef and Italian sausage in an 8-quart stockpot for about 20 minutes or until browned; drain well.
4. Add the sautéed vegetables, rosemary, basil, oregano, bouillon cubes, bay leaf, chili powder, fennel seeds, tomatoes, tomato sauce, water and wine to the stockpot. Simmer for 2 to 3 hours, stirring occasionally.
5. Add the tomato paste, sugar, parsley and cheese. Simmer for 30 to 40 minutes longer.
6. Serve over hot cooked spaghetti.

♩ Also works well as a lasagna sauce.

Prep Time: 20 minutes   Cook Time: 3 1/2 hours   Yield: 8 to 10 servings

Spinach Rice Casserole

Deeply yet delicately flavored spinach is featured with brown rice in this baked side dish.

3 tablespoons butter
1/2 cup chopped onion
1 to 2 garlic cloves, minced
1/2 teaspoon salt
1 pound raw spinach, chopped
2 cups cooked brown rice
2 eggs, beaten
1/2 cup milk
3/4 cups (3 ounces) shredded Cheddar cheese
2 tablespoons chopped parsley
1 tablespoon soy sauce
Nutmeg
Cayenne pepper
2 tablespoons sunflower seeds
Paprika

1. Preheat the oven to 350 degrees. Butter an 8- or 10-inch baking dish.
2. Melt the butter in an 8-quart stockpot over medium heat. Add the onion, garlic and salt. Sauté for about 5 minutes or until the onion is soft. Add the spinach and cook for 2 minutes or until the spinach is wilted.
3. Combine the spinach mixture, rice, eggs, milk, cheese, parsley, soy sauce, nutmeg and cayenne pepper in a bowl and mix well. Spread in the baking dish.
4. Sprinkle the sunflower seeds and paprika on top.
5. Bake, covered, for 35 minutes.

Prep Time: 30 minutes   Cook Time: 35 minutes   Yield: 6 side servings

In 1975, world champion skier Billy Kidd and Larry Mahan, a six-time All-Around World Champion Cowboy, invited a few Pro Rodeo stars to Steamboat for a day of skiing. They had so much fun that the Cowboy Downhill became an annual event each January where over 100 of the best rodeo cowboys compete in a most unusual ski rodeo. Stay clear of the finish line!

Layered Potato & Onion Gratin

The rave reviews for this dish will more than compensate for the effort involved—absolutely fabulous.

1 sprig of fresh rosemary
2 sprigs of fresh parsley
3 sprigs of fresh thyme, or
  $^1/_2$ teaspoon dried thyme
1 bay leaf
1 to 2 garlic cloves, sliced
3 whole garlic cloves
$^1/_2$ teaspoon cracked pepper
  blend
$^1/_4$ onion, thinly sliced
1 quart half-and-half
  (fat-free is ok)
4 tablespoons butter, divided
3 tablespoons all-purpose
  flour

$^1/_4$ teaspoon cayenne pepper
$^1/_4$ teaspoon nutmeg
$^1/_4$ teaspoon turmeric
Salt to taste
3 cups grated gruyère, Swiss
  or Jarlsburg, divided
1 tablespoon olive oil
1$^3/_4$ red onions, thinly sliced
4 russet potatoes, peeled
  and thinly sliced
1 celery root, peeled and
  thinly sliced
2 to 3 garlic cloves, minced
1 sprig fresh rosemary,
  minced

1. Place 1 rosemary sprig, parsley, thyme, bay leaf, sliced garlic, whole garlic, cracked pepper blend, onion and half-and-half in a saucepan. Bring to a boil, watching carefully so that it doesn't boil over the side. Reduce the heat; simmer over low heat for 5 minutes. Turn off the heat and let steep for 30 minutes. Pour through a strainer into a bowl and set aside.
2. Melt 3 tablespoons butter in a saucepan and add the flour. Cook over medium heat for 3 minutes, stirring constantly. Whisk in the half-and-half mixture.
3. Add the cayenne pepper, nutmeg, turmeric and salt to the sauce. Simmer until thickened. Turn off the heat.
4. Whisk 1 cup of the cheese into the sauce. Set aside.
5. Heat the remaining 1 tablespoon butter and olive oil in a large skillet. Cook the red onions over the lowest possible heat for 1 hour, turning several times. Once the onions are soft, increase the heat to medium and cook for about 25 minutes or until well browned, stirring constantly. Set aside.
6. Preheat the oven to 350 degrees. Coat a 2$^1/_2$-quart baking dish with nonstick cooking spray.
7. Layer the potatoes, celery root, caramelized onions, 2 cups cheese, minced garlic, minced rosemary and sauce $^1/_2$ at a time in the prepared baking dish. Top with the remaining 1 cup cheese.
8. Bake for 1 hour to 1 hour and 20 minutes or until the potatoes are soft and the top is brown. Cover if needed to prevent overbrowning.

Prep Time: 40 minutes   Steep Time: 30+ minutes

Cook Time: 3 hours 10 minutes   Yield: 8 to 10 servings

Glazed Rutabagas

A surprisingly tasty dish for the holidays.

1/4 cup margarine
2 medium rutabagas (about 2 pounds), peeled,
   sliced and cut into 1/2-inch cubes
2 tablespoons packed brown sugar
1 teaspoon salt
1 tablespoon water

1. Melt the margarine in a heavy skillet. Add the rutabagas and cook uncovered over medium heat for 10 minutes or until rutabagas are light brown on all sides, stirring frequently.
2. Sprinkle with the brown sugar, salt and water.
3. Simmer, covered, over low heat for about 20 minutes or until tender, stirring occasionally.

♪ This dish goes well with pork and is a nice side to serve with your holiday turkey!

Prep Time: 5 minutes   Cook Time: 30 minutes   Yields: 4 servings

Baked Sweet Potato Fries

Rich in vitamin A, calcium, and potassium, these fries are also terrific sprinkled with cayenne pepper instead of nutmeg.

4 small or 2 medium sweet potatoes
1 tablespoon butter, melted
1 tablespoon olive oil
1/2 teaspoon seasoned salt
Generous dash of nutmeg

1. Preheat the oven to 450 degrees.
2. Peel the sweet potatoes, cut lengthwise into thin wedges and then into halves.
3. Combine the butter and olive oil in a 9x13-inch baking pan. Add the salt and nutmeg. Toss the sweet potatoes in the oil mixture.
4. Bake for 20 to 30 minutes or until brown and tender, stirring once or twice.

Prep Time: 10 minutes   Cook Time: 30 minutes   Yield: 2 to 3 servings

Roasted Winter Vegetables

Celebrate winter with this earthy combination of vegetables.

2 carrots, peeled and cut into $^1/_2$-inch rounds
1 turnip, peeled and cut into $^1/_2$-inch wedges
1 parsnip, peeled and cut into halves lengthwise,
   then into thick slices
1 or 2 onions, peeled and cut into bite-size pieces
2 potatoes, cut into $^3/_4$-inch wedges
$^1/_3$ cup olive oil
4 garlic cloves, chopped
1 or 2 sprigs of fresh rosemary, coarsely chopped
Salt and black pepper
2 small leeks, cleaned, trimmed and cut into
   halves lengthwise
1 bulb sweet fennel, trimmed and cut into bite size pieces
4 to 5 tablespoons balsamic vinegar

1. Preheat the oven to 350 degrees.
2. Place the carrots, turnip, parsnip, onions and potatoes in a shallow 12x17-inch inch roasting pan or a baking dish with 2-inch sides.
3. Mix the olive oil, garlic, rosemary, salt and pepper in a bowl. Pour over the vegetables and toss to coat.
4. Push the vegetables aside and coat the leeks and fennel with the oil mixture. Remove the leeks and fennel to a plate. Set aside.
5. Bake the remaining vegetables for 15 minutes.
6. Add the reserved leeks and fennel and toss. Bake for 40 minutes longer or until the vegetables are light brown and feel soft when pierced with a sharp knife, tossing every 15 minutes.
7. Remove the pan from the oven. Let cool for about 10 minutes. Sprinkle with additional salt and pepper.
8. Add the vinegar and toss. Serve immediately.

Prep Time: $^1/_2$ hour   Cook Time: 1 hour   Yield: 8 servings.

Goat Cheese Soufflés

Rich, wonderfully fresh, and tangy.

3 egg yolks
³/₄ cup buttermilk
3 tablespoons butter
3 tablespoons all-purpose flour
5 to 6 ounces goat cheese, blue cheese, Gorgonzola cheese,
    feta cheese or goat feta cheese, crumbled
¹/₄ cup finely chopped chives or green onions
Salt and freshly ground pepper to taste
5 egg whites
Grated Parmesan

1. Preheat the oven to 375 degrees. Butter 4 small ramekins.
2. Whisk the egg yolks and buttermilk in a large bowl. Heat the butter and flour in a medium saucepan. Cook for 1 minute, stirring constantly. Gradually whisk in the buttermilk mixture. Cook over medium heat for about 2 to 3 minutes or until thick, stirring constantly. Return the mixture to the bowl and let cool. You can make this a few hours ahead and let stand at room temperature.
3. Stir the goat cheese, chives, salt and pepper into the buttermilk mixture.
4. Beat the egg whites in a medium bowl until stiff. Fold into the cheese mixture ¹/₃ at a time. Do not overmix.
5. Divide the mixture equally among the ramekins. Place on a small baking sheet. Top each with Parmesan cheese.
6. Bake for 30 to 35 minutes or until set and golden brown.

Prep Time: 15 minutes   Cook Time: 30 to 35 minutes   Yield: 4 servings

Even though the Festival
Park is buried under snow
and the winter winds blow,
the music continues with the
Winter Concert Series. The
high school and local
churches offer their venues
for a variety of musical
offerings ranging from
classical soloists to big band,
jazz to gospel.

Cranberry Salsa

Cranberry sauce with a KICK!

1 bag (12 ounces) fresh cranberries
1 orange
2 tablespoons minced peeled ginger
$1/2$ cup plus 2 tablespoons sugar, divided
$3/4$ cup water
Juice of 2 limes
$1/2$ bunch cilantro, leaves only, finely chopped
2 to 4 serrano chiles, seeded and minced

1. Process the cranberries in a food processor until finely chopped. Place in a small ceramic or metal bowl. Peel the zest from the orange and mince.
2. Juice the orange. Combine the orange zest with the ginger, $1/2$ cup sugar and water in a small saucepan. Place over medium-high heat. Simmer until reduced to a thick syrup. Pour the syrup over the cranberries.
3. Add the orange juice, lime juice, cilantro, remaining 2 tablespoons sugar and chiles. Stir gently until combined.
4. Chill until ready to serve.

Prep Time: 30 minutes   Yield: 3 cups

French Bread

A recipe that has satisfied hungry Yampa Valley residents for many years.

1¼ cups warm water (105 to 110 degrees)
1 tablespoon sugar
1 tablespoon vegetable or olive oil
1 teaspoon salt
1 package rapid rise yeast
3 to 3½ cups all-purpose flour
1 large egg, lightly beaten

1. Insert the dough hook attachment into a stand mixer. Combine the water, sugar, oil and salt in the bowl of the mixer. Sprinkle with the yeast and stir to dissolve.
2. Add the flour one cup at a time with the mixer at very low speed until all the flour is incorporated. Increase the speed to medium and knead the dough for about 10 minutes or until it is smooth and elastic. The dough should be slightly sticky when pinched between your fingers. Add additional flour one tablespoon at a time as necessary.
3. Shape the dough into a large ball and place in a greased bowl. Place the bowl in a warm location and cover with a dishtowel. Allow the dough to rise for about 45 to 60 minutes or until doubled in bulk.
4. Punch down the dough. Cover and allow to rise for about 30 to 45 minutes or until doubled in bulk.
5. Punch down the dough again and divide into halves. Shape into two long loaves (about 12 inches each) and place in 2 oiled French bread pans. Bread may also be baked on a large oiled baking sheet, but it will spread out more when it rises. Cover the dough with a towel and allow to rise for about 30 minutes or until doubled in bulk. Do not let it over rise or it will collapse.
6. Preheat the oven to 400 degrees.
7. When the bread is ready to bake, lightly brush the tops with a beaten egg. Bake for 20 to 22 minutes or until golden brown.
8. Remove from the pans and cool on a wire rack.

♪ Put a pan of water on the lower rack in the oven during baking for a crispier crust. A good method for getting the dough to rise is to place the dough in the oven with only the light on. The temperature is about right for rising.

Prep Time: 20 minutes   Rise Time: about 2 hours

Cook Time: 20 to 22 Minutes   Yield: 2 loaves

Pesto Corn Bread

An updated version of a classic standard.

2 eggs
$^3/_4$ cup low-fat buttermilk (see sidebar)
$^1/_4$ cup light sour cream
$^1/_4$ teaspoon baking soda
$^3/_4$ teaspoon baking powder
$^3/_4$ teaspoon salt
Several turns of pepper
1 cup yellow cornmeal
1 to 2 teaspoons vegetable oil
$^1/_2$ cup pesto (see note)

1. Preheat the oven to 450 degrees.
2. Mix the eggs, buttermilk and sour cream lightly in a bowl. Add the baking soda, baking powder, salt and pepper and mix well. Add the cornmeal and mix until a loose batter is formed.
3. Heat the oil in a heavy 8-inch skillet, preferably cast-iron, until the oil just begins to smoke (an enameled cast-iron pan will also work). Swirl the skillet to coat the bottom and side. Discard any excess.
4. Pour the batter into the skillet and drop spoonfuls of pesto over the top. Use a knife to swirl the pesto into the batter.
5. Bake on the center oven rack for about 15 to 20 minutes or until firm to the touch. Remove from the oven and let cool for 3 to 5 minutes.
6. Run a knife around the edge of the skillet to loosen. Unmold carefully and cut into wedges. Serve hot.

♪ Pesto is available in grocery stores. To make your own, process $^1/_2$ cup pine nuts, 1 cup packed basil leaves, 1 large garlic clove, $^1/_3$ cup olive oil and $^1/_2$ cup grated Parmesan cheese in a food processor until well puréed. This makes about 1 cup pesto.

Prep Time: 20 minutes   Cook Time: 15 to 20 minutes   Yield: 6 servings

The slightly acidic lactic acid present in buttermilk helps keep baked goods moist by breaking down gluten and also contributes to a rich and creamy texture. While fresh is best, when only a small amount of buttermilk is needed for baking, powdered buttermilk may be added to the dry ingredients, then add the water in with the liquid ingredients, as directed. Store powder in the refrigerator and it can last for years!! A substitute can be made by adding one tablespoon of white vinegar or lemon juice to 1 cup milk, and let stand for 10 minutes or yogurt can also be substituted in a pinch!

Mocha Muffins

This recipe is a decadent combination of chocolate and coffee flavors (sinful for breakfast, great for a snack).

2 cups all-purpose flour
$^1/_2$ cup sugar
1$^1/_2$ teaspoons baking powder
$^1/_2$ teaspoon salt
2 tablespoons unsweetened baking cocoa
2 tablespoons instant coffee, dissolved in
   2 tablespoons hot water
$^3/_4$ cup milk
6 tablespoons canola oil
1 extra-large egg
1$^1/_2$ teaspoons vanilla extract
1 cup (6 ounces) chocolate chips

1. Preheat the oven to 400 degrees. Grease a muffin pan or line with muffin papers.
2. Mix the flour, sugar, baking powder, salt and baking cocoa in a large bowl.
3. Mix the dissolved coffee, milk, canola oil, egg and vanilla in a small bowl.
4. Gently add the egg mixture to the flour mixture. Add the chocolate chips and stir only enough to mix. Do not overmix!
5. Pour or spoon into the prepared pan, filling each $^3/_4$ full. Sprinkle the tops with a pinch of sugar, if desired.
6. Bake for about 20 minutes for regular muffins and for about 12 to 13 minutes for miniature muffins or until a toothpick inserted into the center of a muffin comes out clean.

At sea level, increase the baking powder to 2 teaspoons, reduce the egg to 1 large egg and reduce the baking time by 3 to 5 minutes.

Prep Time: 15 minutes   Cook Time: 20 minutes for regular muffins,

12 to 13 minutes for miniature muffins

Yield: 12 regular muffins, 24 miniature muffins

Chocolate Cheesecake Bars

Developed for a Strings fundraiser, this treat is a combination of two favorite recipes.

$^{1}/_{2}$ cup (1 stick) butter, melted
2 cups finely crushed chocolate wafer cookies or
   chocolate graham crackers
$^{1}/_{4}$ cup sugar
$^{1}/_{2}$ teaspoon cinnamon
1 cup finely chopped walnuts
24 ounces cream cheese, cut into chunks
4 eggs
$1^{1}/_{2}$ cups sugar
1 tablespoon vanilla extract
$^{1}/_{2}$ cup sour cream
6 tablespoons unsweetened baking cocoa

1. Preheat the oven to 350 degrees.
2. Mix the butter, cookie crumbs, sugar, cinnamon and walnuts in a bowl. Reserve
    $1^{1}/_{2}$ cups for the topping and press the rest onto the bottom of an ungreased
    9x13-inch baking pan.
3. Bake for 12 minutes.
4. Combine the cream cheese, eggs, sugar, vanilla, sour cream and baking cocoa in a
    food processor. Process until smooth. Pour over the prepared crust. Sprinkle the
    remaining crumb mixture evenly over the top.
5. Bake for 55 to 60 minutes.
6. Let cool at room temperature and then chill. Cut into squares.

Prep Time: 25 to 30 minutes   Cook Time: 12 minutes crust,

55 to 60 minutes filling   Yield: 35 pieces ($1^{1}/_{2}$x$1^{1}/_{2}$-inch)

Chocolate Raspberry Bars with Coconut

These flavors marry together in a most exquisite fashion!

3/4 cup (1 1/2 sticks) butter, softened
3/4 cup packed brown sugar
1 egg yolk
1/2 teaspoon salt
1 1/2 cups unbleached all-purpose flour
1 jar (12 to 13 ounces) raspberry jam
1/2 cup sweetened shredded coconut
1 cup (6 ounces) chocolate chips

1. Preheat the oven to 350 degrees. Butter a 9x13-inch glass baking dish.
2. Cream the butter and sugar in a bowl with an electric mixer. Mix in the egg yolk, salt and flour. Press the mixture onto the bottom of the baking dish.
3. Bake for 20 minutes or until the crust is light brown.
4. Let the crust cool slightly for 3 to 4 minutes and then carefully spread the jam evenly over the crust. Bake for 5 minutes longer.
5. Remove from oven and immediately sprinkle the coconut and chocolate chips over the hot jam, pressing lightly into the jam.
6. Let the cookies cool completely in the baking dish on a rack before cutting. Wait until the chocolate chips have hardened again.

Prep Time: 20 minutes   Cook Time: 30 minutes   Yield: 2 dozen bar cookies

Steamboat residents take pride in their skiing and ranching heritage by coming together during what are inevitably the coldest five days of the year for the West's oldest Winter Carnival. Downtown, snow sculptures made by high school students adorn the sidewalks, and road crews bring in snow to cover the streets where the Diamond Hitch parade is held, featuring the only high school band in the country that marches on skis. Skijoring events are also held, a tradition dating back to 1915. Skijoring combines horsemanship and skiing skills with a large dose of adrenaline as skiers are pulled through an obstacle course with a horse at about 40 miles per hour.

Peanut Butter & Chocolate Marble Brownies

People who claim they don't like brownies will be pleasantly surprised!

1 cup (2 sticks) butter, at room temperature
1 cup granulated sugar
1 cup packed brown sugar
4 extra-large eggs
$1/4$ cup milk
1 teaspoon vanilla extract
$1^1/2$ cups all-purpose flour
$3/4$ teaspoon baking powder
$1/2$ cup creamy peanut butter
$3/4$ cup peanut butter chips
$1/2$ cup unsweetened baking cocoa, sifted
1 cup (6 ounces) chocolate chips

1. Preheat the oven to 375 degrees. Butter a 9x13-inch glass baking dish and set aside.
2. Cream the butter in a bowl with an electric mixer until fluffy. Add the sugars and beat until well blended. Beat in the eggs, milk and vanilla. Add the flour and baking powder. Mix until smooth but do not overbeat.
3. Pour half the batter into each of 2 bowls. Stir the peanut butter and peanut butter chips into 1 bowl. Stir the baking cocoa and chocolate chips into the other bowl.
4. Spoon the batters alternately into the baking dish, creating a checkerboard pattern, using 8 spoonfuls of each flavor batter. Swirl through the batter with a knife or spatula to create a marble effect.
5. Bake for 35 to 40 minutes or until set and a toothpick inserted in the center comes out clean.
6. Cool completely in the pan on a wire rack. Cut into squares.

 For sea level: increase granulated sugar to $1^1/3$ cups, use large eggs, reduce flour by $1/3$ cup and increase baking powder to 1 teaspoon.

Prep Time: 25 minutes   Cook Time: 35 to 40 minutes   Yield: 24 bars

162

Oatmeal Cookies

Always a comfort to have these cookies handy.

$^1/_2$ cup (1 stick) butter, at room temperature
1 cup sugar
1 egg
1$^1/_2$ cups all-purpose flour
$^1/_2$ teaspoon salt
$^1/_2$ teaspoon baking soda
$^3/_4$ teaspoon cinnamon
$^1/_2$ teaspoon allspice
$^1/_2$ teaspoon ground cloves
$^1/_3$ cup milk
1$^3/_4$ cups rolled oats
$^7/_3$ cup raisins
$^1/_2$ cup chopped walnuts or pecans

1. Preheat the oven to 350 degrees.
2. Cream the butter in a medium bowl with an electric mixer. Beat in the sugar. Add the egg and beat until light and fluffy
3. Sift together the flour, salt, baking soda, cinnamon, allspice and cloves into a bowl. Add the flour mixture and milk alternately to the creamed mixture. Mix in the oats, raisins and walnuts.
4. Drop approximately 1 teaspoon batter for each cookie onto a cookie sheet.
5. Bake for 15 minutes.

Prep Time: 15 minutes   Cook Time: 15 minutes   Yield: 6 dozen per batch

Local children get a day off school during Winter Carnival to participate in and observe a variety of other street and mountain events including ski racing, ski jumping, and shovel racing. Chariot racing at the nearby rodeo grounds is thrilling to watch. The carnival culminates in a much-anticipated night show featuring the world's only "Lighted Man," a skier donned from head to toe with 200 lights and numerous Roman candles that launch from his backpack.

Ricotta Lemon Cheesecake

This is a wonderful dessert to accompany a great Italian dinner.

1 tablespoon unsalted butter
$^1/_2$ cup graham cracker crumbs
6 cups ricotta cheese, drained (not reduced-fat)
$1^1/_2$ cups granulated sugar, divided
6 large or 5 extra-large eggs, separated
2 teaspoons grated lemon zest (1 large lemon)
$^1/_2$ cup all-purpose flour
2 teaspoons vanilla extract
$^1/_2$ cup heavy whipping cream, whipped
Sprinkle of confectioners' sugar
Fresh berries
Bumbleberry Sauce (see recipe on page 47)

1. Preheat the oven to 425 degrees. Butter a 10-inch springform pan and sprinkle the bottom and side with the graham cracker crumbs.
2. Place the ricotta cheese in a food processor and process for 30 seconds. Gradually add 1 cup granulated sugar and the egg yolks, pulsing after each addition. Remove to a mixing bowl. Beat in the lemon zest, flour and vanilla.
3. Whip the egg whites with the remaining $^1/_2$ cup granulated sugar until stiff. Combine with the whipped cream and fold into the ricotta mixture.
4. Pour into the prepared springform pan. Smooth the top.
5. Bake for 10 minutes. Reduce the oven temperature to 350 degrees. Bake for 1 hour. Turn off the oven and let the cheesecake cool with the door closed. Check after turning off the oven to make sure the top of the cheesecake doesn't burn.
6. Chill until serving time.
7. When ready to serve, sprinkle with confectioners' sugar and fresh berries. Drizzle plates with Bumbleberry Sauce.

For almond cheesecake—omit lemon; add $1^1/_2$ teaspoons almond extract to the batter. Scatter $^1/_2$ cup sliced almonds over the top and bake.
For hazelnut cheesecake—omit lemon; mix 1 cup coarsely chopped hazelnuts into the batter, add grated rind of 1 orange and 2 tablespoons orange liqueur.

Prep Time: 35 minutes   Cook Time: 1 hour 10 minutes   Yield: 12 servings

Chocolate Pecan Pie

Easy enough for a beginner, tasty enough for an expert.

1 (unbaked) 9-inch pie shell
$^1/_2$ cup (3 ounces) chocolate chips or
   butterscotch chips
$^1/_2$ cup (1 stick) butter
2 eggs
$^1/_2$ cup all-purpose flour
1 cup chopped pecans
1 cup sugar
1 teaspoon vanilla extract

1. Preheat the oven to 350 degrees.
2. Place the pie shell in a 9-inch pie plate. Spread the chocolate chips over the bottom of the pie shell.
3. Melt the butter in a medium saucepan over medium heat. Remove from the heat and beat in the eggs with a whisk or fork. Stir in the flour, pecans, sugar and vanilla. Mix thoroughly. Pour over the chocolate chips.
4. Bake for 40 to 45 minutes or until set and a knife inserted in the center comes out clean.
5. Cool to room temperature before serving or chill.
6. Serve with whipped cream.

Prep Time: 15 minutes   Cook Time: 40 to 45 minutes

Yield: 6 to 8 servings

Think of champagne, and it conjures up images of lighter than air bubbles. But out west in Colorado, champagne has a whole different meaning—fluffy, dry, white, deep snow. It's the stuff that makes Colorado skiing famous. It's called Champagne. . .and it was first uncorked right here in Steamboat Springs. Local legend says rancher Joe McElroy coined the phrase. Out skiing one sunny day in the early fifties, he turned to a few friends and said the stuff looked like champagne. . . Champagne Powder®.

The term Champagne Powder® snow is the registered trademark of the Steamboat Ski & Resort Corporation and is used by permission.

Champagne Powder®

This coconut sorbet is a very elegant finish to a meal served in martini or saucer Champagne glasses.

1¹/₂ cups boiling water
1¹/₂ cups sweetened shredded coconut
1 cup water
1 cup sugar
Fresh fruit or berries for garnish

1. Pour the boiling water over the coconut in a small bowl. Steep for 4 to 6 hours or overnight.
2. Mix 1 cup water and sugar in a small saucepan. Heat through, stirring constantly until the sugar dissolves. Set aside.
3. Pour the coconut mixture into a blender and purée. Strain the mixture through a fine sieve and discard the solids. Stir in the reserved sugar syrup.
4. Pour into a 7x11-inch or 9x9-inch ceramic or glass freezerproof container. Cover and freeze for about 6 hours or until solid.
5. Remove from the freezer and break into pieces. Purée in a food processor in 2 or 3 batches. Pour into a plastic freezer container; cover and freeze again for about 6 hours or until solid.
6. Serve small scoops in martini or saucer Champagne glasses. Garnish with fresh fruit or berries.

♪ A variation is apricot sorbet. Cover 1¹/₄ cups dried apricots with boiling water and steep for 4 to 6 hours. Purée in a blender. Do not strain, but mix the fruit purée with the sugar syrup and freeze. Purée chunks of the frozen mixture in a food processor and freeze again until solid.

Prep Time: 22 minutes   Steep Time: 4 to 6 hours
Freeze Time: 12 hours, divided   Yield: 2¹/₂ cups

Cranberry Sorbet

1 1/2 cups water, divided
3/4 cup sugar
1 package (12 ounces) cranberries (can be frozen)
1 tablespoon lemon juice
Fresh fruit or berries

1. Mix 3/4 cup water and the sugar in a small saucepan. Heat until the sugar dissolves, stirring constantly. Set aside.
2. Place the cranberries and remaining 3/4 cup water in a large saucepan and bring to a simmer. Cook for 5 minutes or for 10 minutes if the fruit is frozen.
3. Purée the fruit mixture in a blender. Strain through a fine sieve or cheesecloth, discarding any solids. Mix in the lemon juice and reserved sugar syrup.
4. Pour into a 7x11-inch or 9x9-inch ceramic or glass freezerproof container. Cover and freeze for about 6 hours or until solid.
5. Remove from the freezer and break into pieces. Purée in a food processor in 2 or 3 batches. Pour into a plastic freezer container. Cover and freeze again for about 6 hours or until solid.
6. Serve small scoops in martini glasses. Garnish with small slices of fresh fruit or berries. It is fun to serve more than one flavor at a time.

♪ A variation is to purée 3 cups blueberries with 1/2 cup water or 6 kiwifruit, peeled and diced (with no water) to yield 1 1/2 cups fruit purée. Add sugar syrup and lemon juice. Freeze until solid and then break into chunks. Purée in a food processor until smooth and freeze again until firm.

Prep Time: 25 minutes   Cook Time: 5 to 10 minutes   Yield: 2 1/2 to 3 cups sorbet

The Cardboard Classic, held around the ski area's closing day, rewards locals' creativity and spunk as homemade vehicles constructed from cardboard, duct tape, and glue careen down the face of the mountain to a hilarious frenetic finish.

Mai Tai Pineapple

The combination of pineapple and rum conjures up visions of a tropical paradise.

1 pineapple
$^1/_4$ cup dark rum
$^1/_2$ cup shredded coconut, toasted

1. Cut a slice off the bottom of the pineapple and cut off the leafy green top. With the pineapple standing upright, cut off the rind and the eyes. Cut the pineapple lengthwise and then into halves. Cut off the woody core of each piece. Cut each quarter into $^1/_2$-inch wedges; cut each wedge into bite-size pieces.
2. Place the pineapple pieces in a bowl and drizzle with the rum. Let stand for a few minutes or up to 1 hour, stirring occasionally to make sure the rum is well distributed.
3. Serve in bowls. Pouring any rum or juice combination over the pineapple in each bowl. Sprinkle with the shredded coconut.

Prep Time: 10 minutes   Yield: 4 to 6 servings

Chocolate Pecan Bread Pudding

An elegant finale to any dinner.

$^1/_3$ cup dark raisins
$^1/_3$ cup golden raisins
$^1/_4$ cup bourbon, rum or Kahlúa
$^2/_3$ cup chopped pecans
$2^2/_3$ cups milk
3 ounces unsweetened chocolate, finely chopped
5 eggs
$1^1/_3$ cups sugar
1 tablespoon vanilla extract
Pinch of salt
$^1/_4$ teaspoon cloves
1 teaspoon cinnamon
1 teaspoon nutmeg
6 tablespoons unsalted butter, melted and cooled slightly
6 cups day-old French bread, cut into $^1/_2$-inch cubes
Sweetened whipped cream and raspberries for garnish

1. Spray a 9x13-inch pan with nonstick cooking spray and set aside.
2. Combine the raisins and bourbon in a small bowl. Let stand for 30 minutes.
3. Place the pecans in a skillet and toast over medium heat for about 3 to 5 minutes or until fragrant. Set aside.
4. Heat the milk in a saucepan until very hot but not boiling.
5. Combine the chocolate and 1 cup of the hot milk in a bowl; stir until partially melted. Add the remaining milk and continue stirring until incorporated.
6. Beat the eggs, sugar, vanilla, salt, cloves, cinnamon and nutmeg in a large bowl with an electric mixer for about 4 to 5 minutes or until thickened. Beat in the chocolate mixture and melted butter. Stir in the raisin mixture, pecans and bread cubes.
7. Pour into the prepared pan and let stand for 1 hour.
8. Preheat the oven to 350 degrees.
9. Bake, covered loosely with foil, for 30 minutes. Uncover and bake for 25 minutes longer or until the center is set. Remove from the oven and let stand for 1 to 2 hours.
10. Serve warm, at room temperature or chilled with sweetened whipped cream and raspberries.

Prep Time: 45 minutes to 1 hour   Stand Time: 2 to 3 hours

Cook Time: 55 minutes   Yield: 10 servings

Chocolate Soufflés

Everyone receives the royal treatment with these individual soufflés.

2 tablespoons butter
2 tablespoons all-purpose flour
1 cup milk
¼ cup plus 2 tablespoons sugar, divided
8 ounces bittersweet chocolate, chopped
1 ounce unsweetened chocolate, chopped
4 eggs, separated
¼ teaspoon salt
Whipped cream

1. Butter eight 6-ounce ramekins; dust with sugar.
2. Melt the butter in a heavy saucepan over medium heat. Add the flour and cook for about 1 minute or until the mixture is bubbling, stirring constantly. Increase the heat to medium-high and gradually stir in the milk. Cook for 2 to 3 minutes or until mixture thickens and boils, stirring constantly.
3. Remove from the heat. Add ¼ cup sugar and the chocolate, stirring until smooth.
4. Pour the soufflé mixture into a large bowl. Cool to room temperature, stirring occasionally. Stir in egg yolks.
5. Beat the egg whites and salt in medium bowl until soft peaks form. Gradually add the remaining 2 tablespoons sugar; beat until stiff. Fold the egg whites into the soufflé in ⅓ at a time.
6. Divide the soufflé mixture evenly among the prepared ramekins. Cover tightly and freeze for up to 2 weeks.
7. Preheat the oven to 400 degrees.
8. Unwrap the frozen soufflés and place on a baking sheet. Bake for about 22 minutes or until puffed and centers move slightly when shaken gently.
9. Serve immediately with whipped cream.

Prep Time: 30 minutes   Cook Time: 22 minutes   Yield: 8 soufflés

Chocolate Truffles

Delectable, decadent, and sinfully good.

24 ounces good-quality semisweet chocolate chips
1¹/₂ cups heavy cream
2 tablespoons vanilla extract
2 tablespoons almond extract or amaretto
Ground almonds or pecans
Sweetened coconut, lightly toasted in a
    375 degree oven for 7 minutes

1. Place the chocolate chips, cream, vanilla and almond in a medium saucepan or double boiler.
2. Heat over low heat, stirring constantly until the chocolate is fully melted and appears shiny on the surface.
3. Remove to a large dish to cool. Let cool at room temperature for 30 minutes. Remove to the refrigerator or freezer for faster cooling.
4. In 1 hour, or when the chocolate is pliable yet firm (able to be scooped out with a spoon but maintain its shape), scoop out by small spoonfuls. Shape each scoopful into a ball and roll in the nuts or coconut.
5. Store in the refrigerator until the chocoholic in you can't stand it and then serve.

Prep Time: 25 minutes   Yield: 50 truffles

Spring

Annual spring runoff from Mt. Werner fills the banks of the Yampa River.

PHOTOGRAPH BY COREY KOPISCHKE

Dinner for Two

One-Of-A-Kind Lox
182

Exotic Spinach Salad
187

Herbed Rack of Lamb
190

Rosemary Roasted New Potatoes
203

Chocolate Mousse with Cinnamon
Whipped Cream
214

South of the Border Buffet

Guacamole Layered Dip
177

Chile Cheese Bites
179

Cuban Chicken
196

Steamed Rice

Kahlúa Swirl Cake
211

Fish Creek, swollen with snowmelt, charges over the falls and under the bridge of Routt National Forest Trail 1102.

PHOTOGRAPH BY CHRIS SELBY

Appetizers

Soups & Salads

Entrées

Entrées (continued)

Sides & Accompaniments

Breads

Sweets & Desserts

Guacamole Layered Dip

MUSICIAN GENE POKORNY

4 avocados, peeled, cored
  and mashed
Juice of 1 lemon
1 1/2 teaspoons garlic powder
3/4 teaspoon salt, or to taste
1/4 teaspoon pepper, or
  to taste
8 ounces (1 cup) sour cream

3 to 4 green onions, diced
1 tomato, diced
1 cup (4 ounces) shredded
  Monterey Jack cheese
1 cup (4 ounces) shredded
  sharp Cheddar cheese
16 ounces (2 cups) salsa
Tortilla chips

1. Mix the avocados, lemon juice, garlic powder, salt and pepper in a bowl. Spread the mixture over the bottom of an 8x8-inch glass serving dish.
2. Layer the sour cream, green onions, tomato, cheeses and salsa over the avocado mixture.
3. Serve with tortilla chips.

Prep Time: 20 minutes   Yield: 5 to 6 cups

Gene Pokorny is the Principal Tuba for the Chicago Symphony Orchestra. He has played at the Strings in the Mountains Musical Festival as part of the Alpen Brass Ensemble. Gene provided the Guacamole Layered Dip recipe as part of the "optional, additional information" when auditioning for the St. Louis Symphony in 1983. He got the job!

Baked Vidalia Onion Dip

Enjoy the sweet, mild flavor of the new crop of these southern favorites. If Vidalias are unavailable, substitute another sweet onion.

2 tablespoons butter
2 large Vidalia onions,
  coarsely chopped
  (about 5 cups)
6 ounces Swiss cheese,
  shredded (1 1/2 cups)
1 cup mayonnaise

4 ounces sliced water
  chestnuts, drained and
  chopped
1/4 cup dry white wine
1 garlic clove, minced
1/2 teaspoon hot sauce
Tortilla chips or crackers

1. Preheat the oven to 375 degrees. Lightly grease a 2-quart baking dish.
2. Melt the butter in a large skillet over medium-high heat. Sauté the onions for about 10 minutes or until very soft, but not browned.
3. Mix the onions, cheese, mayonnaise, water chestnuts, wine, garlic and hot sauce in a bowl. Pour into the baking dish.
4. Bake for 10 to15 minutes. Let stand for 10 minutes.
5. Serve with tortilla chips or crackers.

Prep Time: 15 minutes   Cook Time: 25 minutes   Yield: 4 cups

Texas Caviar

A tasty, versatile combination of flavors and textures.

1 bunch green onions,
   chopped
1 green bell pepper, diced
2 to 3 jalapeño chiles,
   seeded and minced
2 cans (15 ounces each)
   black-eyed peas, drained
   and rinsed

2 teaspoons minced garlic
2 tomatoes, chopped
2 cans (15 ounces each)
   hominy, drained
   and rinsed
1 bottle (8 ounces) zesty
   Italian salad dressing, or
   1 cup vinaigrette of choice

1. Mix the green onions, bell pepper, jalapeño chiles, black-eyed peas, garlic, tomatoes, hominy and salad dressing in a bowl.
2. Cover and refrigerate for at least 2 hours, preferably overnight.
3. Keeps about 1 week in the refrigerator.

Serving Suggestion: Can be served with chips, in pita halves or as a salad.

Prep Time: 15 minutes   Chill Time: at least 2 hours   Yield: 4 to 5 cups

Marinated Mushrooms & Artichokes

Vegetarian, low-calorie, gluten free—how can anything so healthy taste so good?

1/2 cup tarragon vinegar or
   red wine vinegar
1/4 cup peanut oil
1/4 cup chopped fresh parsley
2 teaspoons salt
1/2 teaspoon thyme
1/2 teaspoon oregano
1/4 teaspoon freshly
   ground pepper

1/8 teaspoon garlic powder
1 pound mushrooms,
   washed and quartered
1 can (14 ounces) artichoke
   hearts, drained and
   quartered
1 red onion, halved
   vertically, sliced thinly,
   and separated into rings

1. Mix the vinegar, oil, parsley, salt, thyme, oregano, pepper and garlic powder in a bowl. Add the mushrooms, artichoke hearts and onion and mix well.
2. Cover and refrigerate for 24 hours, stirring occasionally. Serve with toothpicks.

Prep Time: 10 to 15 minutes   Chill Time: 24 hours   Yield: 4 cups

Chile Cheese Bites

These easy to prepare bites are great for a large group.

2 cups (8 ounces) shredded Monterey Jack cheese
2 cups (8 ounces) shredded Cheddar cheese
3 eggs
1 can (4 ounces) chopped green chiles, or more to taste

1. Preheat the oven to 350 degrees.
2. Mix the cheeses, eggs and green chiles in a bowl and pour into an ungreased 7x12-inch baking dish.
3. Bake for 30 minutes. Cool for 30 minutes or until set.
4. Cut into 1-inch squares and place on tortilla chips, if desired.

Prep Time: 15 minutes   Cook Time: 30 minutes   Yield: 40 (1-inch) pieces

Baked Cambozola

The Sheraton Steamboat Resort offers spectacular slopeside views in a warm western setting. Their restaurants provide something to tantalize all tastes and all ages.

CHEF SCOTT M. KING

1 (4-ounce) bread boule, roll or miniature rustic loaf
3 ounces Cambozola cheese
1 tablespoon brown sugar
$1/2$ tablespoon sun-dried cranberries
$1/2$ tablespoon toasted slivered almonds
Toast points, fruit or crackers

1. Preheat the oven to 300 degrees.
2. Cut the top off the bread and hollow out to form a bread shell, reserving the top.
3. Place the cheese in the bread shell and top with the brown sugar, sun-dried cranberries and almonds.
4. Replace the top on the bread and place on a baking sheet.
5. Bake for about 20 minutes.
6. Remove the top to serve. Spread the melted cheese on toast points, fruit or crackers.

Prep Time: 10 minutes   Cook Time: 20 minutes   Yield: 3 to 4 servings

Crab Cakes

1 egg
1 teaspoon Dijon mustard
1 tablespoon mayonnaise
1/4 teaspoon salt
1 tablespoon chopped
 fresh chives
Pinch of cayenne pepper
1 pound crabmeat, pulled
 into chunks

1/2 cup fine fresh bread
 crumbs
1/2 cup dry bread crumbs
2 tablespoons unsalted
 butter, divided
2 tablespoons olive oil,
 divided
Chipotle Rémoulade
 (see recipe below)

1. Beat the egg in a medium bowl. Add the mustard, mayonnaise, salt, chives and cayenne pepper and mix to incorporate. Add the crabmeat and fresh bread crumbs and mix gently. Spread the dried bread crumbs on a plate.
2. Shape the crab mixture into 1 1/2-inch patties approximately 1/2 inch thick, squeezing to remove any excess liquid.
3. Roll the crab cakes in the dried bread crumbs and arrange in a single layer on a plate or baking sheet. Cover with plastic wrap and refrigerate for at least 1 hour.
4. When ready to cook, heat 1 tablespoon butter and 1 tablespoon oil in a nonstick 10-inch skillet over medium-high heat.
5. Cook half the crab cakes for about 3 to 4 minutes on each side or until golden brown.
6. Place the crab cakes on a baking sheet in a preheated 300-degree oven to keep warm.
7. Add the remaining butter and oil and repeat the cooking procedure for the remaining crab cakes. Serve warm with Chipotle Rémoulade.

Prep Time: 20+ minutes   Chill Time: 1 hour   Cook Time: 8 minutes per batch

Yield: 16 to 20 (1 1/2-inch) cakes

Chipotle Rémoulade

La Montaña has been a tradition for more than 20 years. This award-winning Southwestern and Mexican restaurant is located at the base of the ski area.

CHEF DAMON RENFROE

1 1/2 cups mayonnaise
1/4 cup thinly sliced
 green onions
2 canned chipotle chiles in
 adobo sauce, minced
3/4 cup finely diced celery
3/4 cup minced yellow onion

2 tablespoons lemon juice
1/2 cup ketchup
1/4 cup mustard
1/4 cup whole grain mustard
Salt and pepper to taste
Horseradish to taste

Place all the ingredients in a food processor or blender and purée until mixed well.

Macadamia Nut Shrimp

Marnos Custom Catering specializes in ethnic cuisine, seafood, and Southwestern-style dishes, all made with fresh and seasonal ingredients.

CHEF NANNY MARNO

2 cups macadamia nuts, finely chopped
2 cups panko bread crumbs (Japanese bread crumbs)
1 pound (41- to 50-count) shrimp, peeled and deveined
1 cup all-purpose flour, seasoned with salt and pepper
6 eggs, beaten
Vegetable oil for frying
Spicy Pineapple Sauce (see recipe below)

1. Combine the macadamia nuts and bread crumbs in a bowl.
2. Dip the shrimp in the seasoned flour, then the eggs and then the macadamia breading. Use a small amount of breading at a time to prevent clumping.
3. Pour the oil into a medium skillet to a depth of $1/2$ inch. Preheat the oil to 350 degrees. The shrimp should sizzle when added; if they don't, the oil is not hot enough.
4. Fry the shrimp in batches for about 2 to 3 minutes or until golden brown. Remove with a slotted spoon and drain on paper towels. Shrimp can be prepared to this point, refrigerated and reheated in a preheated 300-degree oven until warm.
5. Serve the shrimp with Spicy Pineapple Sauce.

Prep Time: 30 minutes   Cook Time: 2 to 3 minutes   Yield: 41 to 50 servings

Spicy Pineapple Sauce

Leftover sauce keeps almost indefinitely in the refrigerator.

1 can (20 ounces) juice-pack crushed pineapple
$1/4$ cup sambal oelek (ground fresh chili paste
    available in Asian section of supermarket)
$1/2$ cup rice vinegar
$1/2$ cup sugar

1. Place the undrained pineapple in a food processor and process for three 1-second pulses to lightly purée.
2. Bring the puréed pineapple, sambal oelek, rice vinegar and sugar to a boil in a saucepan, stirring constantly Remove from the heat.

Ilya Kaler is the only violinist ever to win Gold Medals at all three of the world's most prestigious competitions: the Tchaikovsky, the Sibelius, and the Paganini competitions. Dr. Kaler has recently been appointed Professor of Violin at DePaul University. Both Ilya & Olga have performed as part of Strings chamber music concerts.

One-Of-A-Kind Lox

This is the best lox—ever!

MUSICIANS ILYA & OLGA KALER

2 teaspoons diced fresh ginger
2 garlic cloves
1/4 cup loosely packed fresh dill
Grated zest of 1/2 lemon
Grated zest of 1/2 orange
1/4 cup citron-flavored vodka
1/4 cup kosher salt
1 (1-pound) salmon fillet, even thickness, skinned,
    pin bones removed, rinsed and patted dry

1. Line an 8x8-inch glass baking dish with plastic wrap, leaving an extra 6 inches at both ends.
2. Prepare the marinade by combining the ginger, garlic, dill, lemon zest and orange zest in a food processor. Add the vodka and salt and pulse to blend.
3. Place half the marinade in the prepared dish; top with the salmon and remaining marinade. Wrap sides and ends of plastic wrap around the salmon, sealing tightly.
4. Place a heavy pan 6 inches in diameter on top of the wrapped fish and weight it down with a 1-pound or heavier can. Place in the refrigerator for 24 to 36 hours.
5. Wash thoroughly. If the salmon seems too salty, soak in cold water for 10 minutes. Slice thinly against the grain.

Serving Suggestion: Serve lox with thinly sliced baguette or water crackers accompanied by cream cheese and mustard sauce.

Prep Time: 20 minutes   Chill Time: 24 hours   Yield: 6 to 8 servings

Mustard Sauce

1/4 cup stone-ground mustard
1 teaspoon dry mustard
3 tablespoons sugar
2 tablespoons white vinegar
3 tablespoons fresh dill
1/3 cup vegetable oil

1. Combine the mustards, sugar, vinegar and dill in a food processor and process until smooth. Slowly add the oil while processing.
2. The sauce is better if made the day before and will keep in the refrigerator for at least a week.

Black Bean & Roasted Tomato Soup

Catamount Ranch and Club is a private eighteen-hole golf club with a restaurant open to the public. Enjoy this delicious soup from their restaurant.

CHEF SAM GORDON

$^1/_2$ cup (1 stick) butter
2 onions, diced
2 carrots, peeled and diced
2 ribs celery, diced
2 cups tequila
1 can (15 ounces) black beans, drained
1 can (15 ounces) fire-roasted tomatoes
    (available at most supermarkets)
4 cups chicken or vegetable stock
1 pint (2 cups) heavy cream
Salt and freshly ground pepper to taste
Sour cream
Chives, minced

1. Melt the butter in a large stockpot over medium heat. Add the onions, carrots and celery and sauté until translucent and soft.
2. Carefully add the tequila away from the flame and return to the heat. Cook for 5 minutes, stirring constantly.
3. Add the black beans and tomatoes and bring to a simmer, stirring occasionally.
4. Add the stock and bring to a slow boil. Reduce the heat to low and simmer for 45 minutes.
5. Purée the soup in a blender in small batches until smooth (optional). Return to the stockpot.
6. Add the heavy cream and bring the mixture back to a simmer. Add salt and pepper.
7. Serve garnished with sour cream and minced chives.

Prep Time: 10 to 15 minutes   Cook Time: 1 hour   Yield: 4 to 6 servings

Tortilla Soup

Blue Bonnet Catering offers haute cuisine to hoedown.

CHEF MELISSA CARTAN

2 tablespoons olive oil
$^1/_2$ red onion, chopped
2 tablespoons chopped garlic
1 red bell pepper, chopped
2 cans (4 ounces each) diced green chiles
1 can (15 ounces) corn, drained
1 can (15 ounces) black beans, rinsed and drained
4 cups water
1 tablespoon chili powder
1 teaspoon cumin
1 tablespoon salt
1 teaspoon freshly ground black pepper
Pinch of cayenne pepper
1 can (28 ounces) diced tomatoes
1 small jalapeño chile
$^1/_2$ bunch cilantro, stem ends removed
Tortilla chips, broken into pieces

1. Heat the olive oil in a stockpot. Add the onion, garlic, and bell pepper and sauté for about 5 minutes or until softened.
2. Add the green chiles, corn, black beans, water, chili powder, cumin, salt, black pepper and cayenne pepper and bring to a boil.
3. Process the tomatoes, jalapeño chile and cilantro in a blender.
4. Add the tomato mixture to the boiling mixture in the stockpot.
5. Reduce the heat to low and simmer for 30 minutes.
6. Sprinkle a handful of tortilla chips in a cup or bowl and ladle the soup over the chips. Serve immediately.

Prep Time: 30 to 40 minutes   Cook Time: 30 minutes   Yield: 4 servings

Crab & Lobster Bisque

A Catered Affair meets the clients' wishes from a unique cookie basket to multiple course sit-down dining.

CHEF MARCEE MARIE

7 tablespoons butter, divided
6 tablespoons chopped onion
1/4 cup minced celery
2 tablespoons minced shallots
5 tablespoons all-purpose flour
3 cups light cream
2 cups chicken stock
1/2 cup dry white wine
1/2 teaspoon salt
1/2 teaspoon white pepper
1 pound crabmeat, lobster or shrimp, or
   a combination of each, shells removed
1/2 cup brandy
Paprika
1/2 cup minced chives
4 to 8 crostini

1. Melt 5 tablespoons butter in a heavy 5-quart saucepan over medium heat. Add the onions, celery and shallots and sauté for 5 minutes.
2. Sprinkle the flour over the vegetables and cook for 3 minutes, stirring constantly.
3. Gradually add the cream, chicken stock and wine. Cook until smooth and slightly thickened, stirring constantly. Season with the salt and white pepper and reduce the heat to a simmer.
4. Melt the remaining 2 tablespoons butter in a skillet over medium heat. Add the crabmeat and cook for 5 minutes or until warmed through, stirring occasionally.
5. Heat the brandy to the boiling point in a small saucepan and pour over the crabmeat.
6. Stir the crab mixture into the cream sauce. Cover and simmer for 10 minutes.
7. Purée the bisque in a blender or food processor in batches and return to the saucepan.
8. Ladle into bowls and garnish with paprika and minced chives.
9. Serve with the crostini.

Prep Time: 15 minutes   Cook Time: 35 minutes   Yield: 4 servings

Asparagus Salad

1 pound asparagus, tough ends removed
6 to 8 cups salad greens
2 eggs, hard-cooked and sliced
1/4 cup finely chopped red bell pepper
White Wine and Dijon Vinaigrette Dressing (see below)

1. Cook the asparagus in boiling water in a saucepan for 7 minutes. Remove from the heat and plunge into cold water to stop the cooking process and preserve the brilliant green color.
2. Place the salad greens on individual plates and arrange the cooled asparagus on top. Arrange the eggs on top of the asparagus and sprinkle with the bell pepper.
3. Drizzle with the vinaigrette.

Prep Time: 10 minutes   Yield: 6 to 8 servings

White Wine and Dijon Vinaigrette

1/3 cup extra-virgin olive oil
3 tablespoons white wine vinegar
3 tablespoons minced shallots
1 1/4 teaspoons Dijon mustard
1/2 teaspoon salt
Freshly ground pepper to taste

Combine the olive oil, vinegar, shallots, mustard, salt and pepper in a bowl and whisk until blended. Or combine the ingredients in a jar with a tight-fitting lid and shake to blend just before drizzling over the salad.

When selecting asparagus, choose spears with compact firm tips and rich green stalks. Cook as soon as possible after purchasing. To store for a few days, treat asparagus as you would fresh flowers. Trim the stems and place them upright in a glass with a few inches of water. Cover loosely with a plastic bag and keep in the refrigerator. Thin stalks are attractive in stir fries and as garnishes while thicker stalks work well for roasting and grilling.

Exotic Spinach Salad

So beautiful it deserves center stage!

8 cups rinsed, torn spinach
1 papaya, cut into $^1/_2$-inch pieces
1 mango, cut into $^1/_2$-inch pieces
1 kiwifruit, sliced
1 cup strawberries, sliced
Fruit Salad Dressing (see recipe below)
Edible flowers (optional) –from your garden or
   available in the specialty section of the supermarket

1.   Combine the spinach, papaya, mango, kiwifruit and strawberries in a bowl.
2.   Pour the salad dressing over the salad and toss to coat. Top with edible flowers.

Prep Time: 25 minutes   Yield: 8 servings

Fruit Salad Dressing

$^1/_3$ cup sugar
2 tablespoons sesame seeds
1 tablespoon poppy seeds
$1^1/_2$ teaspoons grated onion
$^1/_4$ teaspoon Worcestershire sauce
$^1/_4$ teaspoon paprika
$^1/_4$ cup cider vinegar
$^1/_2$ cup vegetable oil

Combine the sugar, sesame seeds, poppy seeds, onion, Worcestershire sauce, paprika and vinegar in a blender. Add the oil slowly and process until the dressing is moderately thick.

For a colorful and stylish presentation, garnish dishes with edible flower blossoms, including: bee balm, begonia, calendula, chive blossom, chrysanthemum, dandelion, daylily, dianthus/pinks, English daisy, hollyhock, hyssop, lavender, lilac, nasturtium, pansy, rose, rose-of-sharon, sweet woodruff, tulip and violet. Choose flowers early in the day and only those that are pesticide free.

Roasted Red Pepper Salad

Olive oil
6 red bell peppers, halved
2 tablespoons red wine vinegar
2 tablespoons olive oil
Salt and freshly ground pepper to taste
2 garlic cloves, chopped
2 green onions, sliced

1. Preheat the broiler.
2. Rub olive oil on the bell pepper halves. Place cut side down on a baking sheet and broil until the skins are charred.
3. Remove the bell peppers from the oven and place in a plastic bag for 15 minutes. Remove the charred skins and cut the bell peppers into strips.
4. Combine the red wine vinegar, 2 tablespoons olive oil, salt, pepper, garlic and green onions in a jar with a tight-fitting lid. Cover and shake well.
5. Place the bell peppers in a serving dish and pour the dressing over the top.

Prep Time: 30 minutes   Yield: 8 to 10 servings

Chicken Salad

*The addition of dried cherries and raisins elevates this salad from
Blue Bonnet Catering to another level.*

CHEF MELISSA CARTAN

1 rotisserie chicken, skinned, deboned and shredded
1/4 cup chopped red onion
3 ribs celery, chopped
1/2 cup toasted pecans
1/2 cup golden raisins
1/2 cup sundried cherries
1 1/2 cups mayonnaise
Salt and pepper, to taste

Combine the chicken, onion, celery, pecans, raisins, cherries, mayonnaise, salt and pepper in a bowl and mix well. This will keep in the refrigerator for several days.

Prep Time: 15 minutes   Yield: 6 to 8 servings

Dijon Leg of Lamb

A sophisticated entrée, perfect for entertaining.

1 whole leg of lamb (about 6 pounds), or
   1 boneless leg of lamb (about 4 pounds)
2 garlic cloves, each sliced into 3 or 4 pieces
1 tablespoon Dijon mustard
1 tablespoon plus 1 cup strong coffee, divided
2 teaspoons ground ginger
1/4 cup sweet sherry or white port wine
1/4 cup chicken stock
4 teaspoons arrowroot or cornstarch
1/4 cup cold water
2 teaspoons butter (optional)

1. Preheat the oven to 350 degrees.
2. Trim the excess fat from the lamb. For a boneless roast, remove the string webbing, remove the excess fat and then tie into an even oval with two lengths of butcher's twine. Cut 6 to 8 small slits in the lamb and insert the garlic slices.
3. Mix the mustard, 1 tablespoon coffee and ginger in a bowl. Rub over the entire surface of the lamb.
4. Mix 1 cup coffee and wine in a bowl.
5. Place the lamb in a shallow roasting pan. Roast for about 1 1/2 to 2 hours or to an internal temperature of 135 degrees for medium-rare, basting with the coffee mixture and pan juices several times during the last hour of roasting. Roast a boneless roast for about 1 hour and 40 minutes.
6. Remove the roast to a warm platter and cover loosely with foil.
7. Spoon fat from the roasting pan. Add any remaining basting mixture and stock to the roasting pan. Bring to a boil, stirring to incorporate the meat particles from the pan. Mix the arrowroot with the cold water and whisk into the sauce. Simmer until thickened, stirring constantly. Enrich the sauce with butter, if desired.

Prep Time: 15 minutes   Cook Time: 1 1/2 to 2 hours   Yield: 10 to 12 servings

Colorado ranks fifth in the nation for sheep and lamb production. The state's clean air and plentiful grazing pastures contribute, not only to the high quality and flavorful meat, but also to the exceptional caliber of wool.

Herbed Rack of Lamb

A pleasant change of flavors for this delicate cut of meat.

4 garlic cloves, minced
1 sprig of fresh rosemary, minced
2 teaspoons oregano
1 teaspoon mint
1 teaspoon parsley
1/4 cup olive oil
2 lamb racks, trimmed
1 cup red wine
Garlic salt to taste
Lemon pepper to taste

1. Combine the garlic, rosemary, oregano, mint, parsley and olive oil in a bowl and mix well. Rub the entire mixture over both sides of the lamb.
2. Place the lamb in a sealable plastic bag and add the wine. Seal the bag and marinate in the refrigerator overnight, turning occasionally.
3. Remove the lamb from the marinade and season with garlic salt and lemon pepper. Discard the remaining marinade.
4. Preheat the grill. Place the lamb on a grill rack. Grill over medium heat for about 25 minutes for medium-rare to medium or to desired degree of doneness, turning occasionally.

Prep Time: 10 minutes   Marinate Time: Overnight   Cook Time: 25 minutes

Yield: 4 servings

Veal & Mushroom Stew

The delicate flavor of veal makes this light stew a perfect dish for Spring.

$^1/_2$ cup all-purpose flour
2 teaspoons salt
$^1/_4$ teaspoon freshly ground pepper
$2^1/_2$ pounds veal cutlets, cut into narrow 3-inch strips
$^1/_4$ cup olive oil
$^1/_2$ cup minced onion
12 ounces fresh mushrooms, chopped
1 can (28 ounces) diced tomatoes with juice
1 teaspoon sugar
1 teaspoon dry mustard
1 tablespoon paprika
3 tablespoons minced fresh parsley
1 tablespoon oregano
Grated Parmesan cheese
Hot cooked rice or noodles

1. Preheat the oven to 350 degrees.
2. Combine the flour, salt and pepper in a shallow bowl and mix well. Add the veal and roll lightly to coat.
3. Heat the olive oil in a large skillet over medium heat. Add the onion and mushrooms and sauté until tender. Remove to a large bowl.
4. Sauté the veal in the remaining drippings in the skillet until brown, adding additional olive oil as needed to prevent sticking. Add to the mushroom mixture. Stir in the undrained tomatoes, sugar, mustard, paprika, parsley and oregano.
5. Pour into a 2-quart baking dish and top with grated cheese.
6. Cover and bake for 45 minutes or until tender.
7. Serve over rice or noodles.

Prep Time: 30 minutes   Cook Time: 45 minutes   Yield: 8 servings

Pork Tenderloin with Cherry Sauce

The sweet, tart sauce is heavenly with lean and versatile pork tenderloin.

2 tablespoons olive oil
2 pork tenderloins (1 pound each)
Cherry Sauce (see recipe below)

1. Heat the olive oil in a large skillet over high heat. Brown the pork on all sides. Reduce the heat to medium. Cook, turning once or twice, for about 10 to 15 minutes or until an instant-read thermometer inserted into the thickest part of the tenderloin registers 150 to 155 degrees. Let stand for 15 minutes to finish cooking (the temperature will continue to rise 5 to 10 degrees).
2. Cut the tenderloin into 1/2-inch slices. Place on a serving platter and top with Cherry Sauce.

Prep Time: 10 minutes   Cook Time: 10 to 15 minutes   Stand Time: 15 minutes

Yield: 6 to 8 servings

Cherry Sauce

1/2 cup cranberry juice or cranberry juice cocktail
1/2 cup port or sherry
3 tablespoons brown sugar
1/2 teaspoon tarragon
1/4 cup dried cherries
1 tablespoon balsamic vinegar
1 tablespoon cornstarch, dissolved in 2 tablespoons cold water

1. Combine the cranberry juice, wine, brown sugar, tarragon, cherries and vinegar in a medium saucepan. Bring to a boil and simmer, covered, for 5 minutes. Add the dissolved cornstarch and cook for 1 minute or until thickened, stirring constantly.
2. This sauce can be made a day ahead and slowly reheated, adding a small amount of water if necessary.

♪ The Cherry Sauce is also great over sautéed boneless chicken breasts or roasted duck.

Prep Time: 5 minutes   Cook Time: 10 minutes   Yield: 1 1/4 cups

Pork Chops with Mustard Cream Sauce

A quick entrée for a family dinner, yet elegant enough for company.

8 pork chops, or 2 pork tenderloins (see sidebar)
Salt and freshly ground pepper to taste
1/4 cup olive oil
1/2 cup dry white wine
1/2 cup heavy cream
1/2 cup spicy brown or Dijon mustard
Chopped fresh parsley

1. Preheat the oven to 250 degrees. Season the pork chops with salt and pepper on both sides.
2. Heat the oil in a large heavy skillet over medium-high heat. Add the pork chops and cook for about 5 minutes on each side or until brown and nearly cooked through but not dry. Place the pork chops on an ovenproof platter and place in the oven to finish and keep warm.
3. Add the wine to the drippings in the skillet, stirring to deglaze the skillet by scraping up the browned bits. Reduce the heat and stir in the cream and mustard until blended well. Cook for 1 or 2 minutes.
4. Pour over the pork chops and garnish with chopped parsley.

If using pork tenderloin,
1. Sauté 2 tenderloins (1 to 1 1/2 pounds each) in hot oil, turning to brown on all sides, about 6 to 7 minutes total.
2. Remove from the skillet and place on an ovenproof baking sheet in a preheated 400-degree oven. Roast for about 10 minutes or until the internal temperature registers about 145 degrees.
3. Make the sauce in the skillet while the pork is finishing. Let rest for about 5 minutes before slicing into 1/2-inch pieces. Place on a serving platter and top with the sauce.

Prep Time: 10 minutes   Cook Time: 15 minutes   Yield: 8 Servings

Strings in the Mountains' early concerts were held in a small room and on the outside deck of the now-defunct Steamboat Athletic Club. On opening night, organizers hoped for at least 50 people to come. To their astonishment, 250 music lovers arrived and squeezed into the small space. The audience played an integral part in these early performances, holding music sheets in the gusty wind and helping move the grand piano around the very small stage. After four years in these cramped quarters, the festival moved to a seasonal tent at the base of the ski area where it remained for twelve years.

Almond-Crusted Chicken Breasts

This smells wonderful while it is baking.

4 boneless skinless chicken breasts
1 cup Lemon Garlic Buttermilk Dressing (see recipe below)
1 cup roasted unsalted whole almonds
2 ounces asiago cheese

1. Preheat the oven to 375 degrees.
2. Place the chicken in a single layer in a shallow dish. Pour the dressing over the chicken, turning several times to coat. Cover with plastic wrap and marinate in the refrigerator for 30 minutes, turning 2 or 3 times.
3. Process the almonds and cheese in a food processor or blender until ground into a coarse meal. Remove to a shallow plate.
4. Lightly grease a shallow baking dish or spray with nonstick cooking spray. Remove the chicken from the marinade, roll in the almond mixture and arrange in a single layer in the baking dish.
5. Bake for 30 to 40 minutes or until the juices run clear.

Prep Time: 10 minutes   Marinate Time: 30 minutes

Cook Time: 30 to 40 minutes   Yield: 4 servings

Lemon Garlic Buttermilk Dressing

$^1/_3$ cup canola or safflower oil
$^1/_4$ cup fresh lemon juice
$^1/_4$ cup mayonnaise
3 tablespoons buttermilk
2 large garlic cloves, pressed
$^3/_4$ teaspoon dill weed
$^3/_4$ teaspoon sugar
$^1/_2$ teaspoon salt
$^3/_4$ teaspoon coarsely ground black pepper

Place all ingredients in a jar with a tight-fitting lid. Cover and shake well.

Yield: 1 cup

Chicken Joe

Spices and pepperoncini contribute to the robust flavor of this bold and colorful dish.

1 teaspoon salt
1/2 teaspoon freshly ground black pepper
2 teaspoons oregano
3/4 teaspoon red pepper flakes
1 chicken, cut into serving pieces
2 tablespoons olive oil
1/2 red bell pepper, cut into broad strips or chunks
1/2 yellow bell pepper, cut into broad strips or chunks
8 to 10 mild pepperoncini, or to taste, drained, rinsed
   and left whole
1 lemon, cut into halves
1/4 cup white wine

1. Preheat the oven to 450 degrees.
2. Mix the salt, black pepper, oregano and red pepper flakes in a small bowl. Sprinkle half the mixture over the skin side of each chicken piece.
3. Heat the oil in a roasting pan or shallow baking dish over medium-high heat. Add the chicken pieces skin side down. Sprinkle the remaining seasoning mixture over the top of the chicken. Bake for about 20 minutes or until the chicken pieces begin to brown.
4. Remove the pan from the oven. Turn the chicken pieces over and add the bell peppers and pepperoncini. Return to the oven and bake for 20 to 30 minutes longer or until the chicken is tender and the pepper strips are soft.
5. Remove the pan from the oven. Squeeze the juice from the lemon halves over the chicken pieces and remove to a warm serving platter.
6. Pour the wine into the pan drippings. Cook for a couple of minutes, stirring to deglaze the pan to loosen the browned bits. Spoon over the chicken.

Pepperoncini is also known as Tuscan, sweet Italian, or golden Greek peppers. They are usually sold pickled and can be found in the condiment section of the supermarket. Used in both Greek and Italian cooking, pepperoncini are popular additions to salads and antipasto platters.

Prep Time: 20 minutes   Cook Time: 40 to 50 minutes   Yield: 4 servings

Cuban Chicken

An eclectic combination of ingredients creates intriguing flavors.

4 boneless skinless chicken breasts
Salt and freshly ground pepper
3 tablespoons olive oil, divided
2 tablespoons butter
1 shallot, chopped
1 garlic clove, minced
2 cups steamed fresh green beans
1/2 cup sliced black olives
1/2 cup raisins or dried cherries
1/4 cup white wine
1/4 cup chicken broth
1/2 teaspoon cumin
1/2 teaspoon cinnamon
1/3 cup slivered almonds, toasted
2 Roma tomatoes, diced
2 tablespoons drained capers

1. Season the chicken with salt and pepper.
2. Heat 1 tablespoon olive oil in a large skillet over medium heat. Add the chicken and sauté for about 5 minutes per side or until browned and no longer pink in the center. Remove the chicken and keep warm.
3. Melt the butter with the remaining olive oil in the skillet. Add the shallot and garlic and cook for 2 minutes.
4. Add the green beans, black olives and raisins and cook for about 3 minutes.
5. Add the white wine and chicken broth and simmer for 5 minutes.
6. Add the cumin, cinnamon, almonds, tomatoes and capers and simmer the sauce for about 10 minutes. Return the chicken to the skillet and simmer for 1 to 2 minutes to heat through.

Serving Suggestion: Serve with rice and a fresh spring salad.

Prep Time: 10 minutes   Cook Time: 30 minutes   Yield: 4 servings

Broiled Salmon Fillet

This is a no-fail way to cook salmon. It works for fillets of any size, making an easy entrée for a dinner party.

1 salmon fillet, boned
Olive oil
Paprika or lemon pepper
Salt and freshly ground pepper
Lemon wedges or Fruit Salsa (see recipe below)

1. Preheat the broiler.
2. Place the salmon skin side down on a rack in a broiler pan or on a baking sheet. Brush with olive oil and dust with paprika. Season with salt and pepper.
3. Broil on the middle oven rack until the fish flakes easily with a fork. You may bake in a preheated 350-degree oven. A $1/2$-inch fillet will be done in 20 minutes and a 1-inch fillet will be done in 20 to 22 minutes.
4. Slice and serve with lemon wedges or Fruit Salsa.

Serving Suggestion: Serve with a green salad and a loaf of good fresh bread.

Prep Time: 5 minutes   Cook Time: 20 to 22 minutes

Yield: 4 to 6 ounces per serving

Fruit Salsa

This tangy salsa works well with fish, chicken, or pork.

1 ripe mango, papaya or peach, peeled and chopped
$1/2$ to 1 teaspoon curry powder (optional)
2 teaspoons olive oil
2 teaspoons finely chopped fresh ginger
2 green onions, finely sliced
$1/4$ cup chopped walnuts (optional)

Mix all the ingredients together in a small bowl. Let stand for a few minutes for the flavors to blend.

Prep time: 10 minutes   Yield: 1 cup

Ripe mangoes have a good combination of yellow, red, and green colors and are slightly soft to the touch. Partially green mangoes will ripen at room temperature, especially if placed in a paper bag. Removing the large seed of this fruit presents a challenge, but perseverance and practice will pay off in the long run! Cut around the flat seed with a sharp knife to separate it from the flesh. The thick peel can easily be removed with a vegetable peeler.

Spicy Roasted Salmon

For taste buds longing for the flavor of barbecue.

1/4 cup pineapple juice
2 tablespoons fresh
    lemon juice
1 1/4-pound salmon fillet
2 tablespoons brown sugar
4 teaspoons chili powder

2 teaspoons grated
    lemon zest
1/4 teaspoon
    cinnamon
3/4 teaspoon cumin
1/2 teaspoon salt

1. Combine the pineapple juice, lemon juice and salmon in a sealable plastic bag
    and marinate in the refrigerator for 1 hour.
2. Preheat the oven to 400 degrees. Line a 7x11-inch baking dish with foil.
3. Remove the fish the from bag and place skin side down in the baking dish. Discard
    the marinade.
4. Mix the brown sugar, chili powder, lemon zest, cinnamon, cumin and salt in a small
    bowl and pat the entire mixture onto the fish.
5. Bake for 15 to 20 minutes or until the fish flakes easily with a fork.

Prep Time: 10 minutes   Marinate Time: 1 hour   Cook Time: 15 to 20 minutes

Yield: 3 to 4 servings

Thai Scallops with Basil

*Control the heat in this easy stir-fry by using red bell pepper in
place of the red chile peppers.*

1/2 pound large sea scallops
2 tablespoons vegetable oil
    (less with nonstick pan)
3 garlic cloves, chopped
1/2 cup canned straw
    mushrooms, drained, or
    sliced fresh mushrooms
1/2 cup shredded bamboo
    shoots

3 tablespoons oyster sauce
2 to 4 red chile peppers,
    seeded and chopped, or
1/2 cup thin strips red bell
    pepper
15 fresh basil leaves
2 cups shredded cabbage or
    steamed white rice

1. Rinse and score the scallops crosswise. Set aside.
2. Heat the oil and garlic on high heat In a wok or large skillet until the garlic bubbles.
    Add the scallops, mushrooms, bamboo shoots, oyster sauce and red chile peppers.
    Stir-fry for 5 minutes or until the scallops are cooked.
3. Stir in the basil. Serve over a bed of shredded cabbage or steamed rice.

Prep Time: 20 minutes   Cook Time: 6 minutes   Yield: 2 servings

Mexican Spaghetti Roberto

Jalapeño chiles give special zest to this carbonara dish.

2 tablespoons olive oil, divided
8 ounces mushrooms, sliced
1 pound bacon, cut into 1-inch squares
3 yellow onions (about 1 1/2 pounds), coarsely chopped
1 tablespoon minced garlic
2 small jalapeño chiles, minced
3/4 cup chicken stock
1 pound ham, cut into 1-inch cubes
1 1/2 pounds uncooked spaghetti
2 eggs
1/2 cup heavy cream
1 cup (4 ounces) freshly grated Parmesan cheese

1. Heat 1 tablespoon olive oil in a 12-inch sauté pan. Add the mushrooms and sauté for about 5 minutes or until soft. Remove the mushrooms and set aside.
2. Cook the bacon in the same pan for about 10 minutes. Drain half the bacon drippings from the pan. Add the onion and sauté until soft and beginning to brown. Add the garlic and chiles and sauté for 2 minutes longer. Add the stock, ham and mushrooms and simmer for 20 minutes.
3. Cook the spaghetti in boiling water with the remaining 1 tablespoon olive oil in a saucepan. Drain but do not rinse.
4. Mix the eggs and cream in a serving bowl. Add the hot spaghetti very slowly to the mixture, stirring constantly. The mixture will curdle if the spaghetti is added too quickly.
5. Pour the ham sauce on top of the spaghetti without mixing in. Sprinkle with the Parmesan cheese.

Prep Time: 45 minutes   Cook Time: 35 minutes   Yield: 8 servings

Linguini with White Clam Sauce

Simple, low-fat ingredients produce a rich and creamy flavor for this classic pasta sauce.

Before the streets were paved, Steamboat Springs melted from a pristine winter wonderland to a muddy mess in the spring. Although most streets in town are now paved, locals take advantage of the quiet time fondly referred to as "mud season." Some people opt for a sunny and warm getaway, while others stay put and prepare the garden, hike the core trail along the river, or simply behold the tender emergence of green from the whiteness of winter.

4 ounces linguini
1^1/2 tablespoons olive oil
^{1}/2 cup finely diced onion
3 garlic cloves, finely diced
1^1/2 teaspoons all-purpose flour
2 cans (6^1/2 ounces each) chopped clams
^{1}/2 cup (2 ounces) freshly grated Parmesan cheese
1 tablespoon minced parsley

1. Cook the linguini using the package directions. Rinse in cold water and drain.
2. Heat the olive oil in large heavy skillet over medium heat. Add the onion and garlic and sauté for about 3 minutes or until soft, adding some of the clam juice if the mixture begins to stick.
3. Blend in the flour and cook for 30 seconds, stirring constantly.
4. Add the undrained clams and cook for 4 minutes longer, stirring constantly.
5. Stir in the cheese. Add the cooked linguini and cook for 1 minute longer, tossing well.
6. Mix in the parsley and serve.

Prep Time: 10 minutes   Cook Time: 20 to 25 minutes   Yield: 2 servings

Spicy Asparagus

Asian-flavored sauce combined with crisp asparagus create a dynamic taste sensation!

6 or 7 garlic cloves, chopped
1 (1-inch) piece fresh ginger, peeled and grated
3/4 teaspoon salt, divided
1 pound asparagus, tough ends removed,
   cut into 2-inch pieces
2 green onions, chopped
1/2 teaspoon sugar
2 1/2 tablespoons soy sauce
1 teaspoon toasted sesame oil
1 tablespoon rice vinegar
1/2 teaspoon hot pepper flakes in oil (caution: very hot)
1/4 teaspoon freshly ground black pepper

1. Combine the garlic, ginger and 1/4 teaspoon salt. Crush into a coarse paste.
2. Boil just enough water in a saucepan to cover the asparagus. Add the asparagus and cook for 2 to 3 minutes or until the asparagus turns bright green.
3. Drain the asparagus and place in a bowl. Mix the garlic paste, green onions, sugar, remaining 1/2 teaspoon salt, soy sauce, sesame oil, rice vinegar, hot pepper flakes and black pepper in a bowl and pour over the asparagus.
4. Serve warm or chilled.

Prep Time: 20 minutes   Cook Time: 2 to 3 minutes   Yield: 4 to 6 servings

Herbed Green Beans

A favorite vegetable taken to another level.

2 cups water
1 pound fresh green beans,
   ends trimmed
$1/2$ teaspoon basil
$1/2$ teaspoon marjoram
$1/2$ teaspoon chives
$1/4$ teaspoon thyme
2 tablespoons vegetable oil

1 small onion,
   finely chopped
1 garlic clove, minced
1 teaspoon salt
$1/2$ teaspoon freshly ground
   pepper
$1/2$ cup sunflower seeds or
   toasted almonds

1. Bring the water to a boil in a saucepan. Add the beans and cook, tightly covered, for 12 to 15 minutes or until tender-crisp.
2. Mix the basil, marjoram, chives and thyme in a small bowl.
3. Heat the oil in a large skillet over medium heat. Sauté the onion and garlic in the oil for 3 to 5 minutes or until tender, adding the herbs near the end.
4. Drain the beans and add to the onion mixture. Season with salt and pepper and toss lightly. Sprinkle with the sunflower seeds.
5. Serve immediately.

Prep Time: 20 minutes   Cook Time: 15 minutes   Yield: 6 servings

Lemon Zucchini

Quick to prepare in the microwave.

4 small zucchini,
   thinly sliced
2 tablespoons water
1 tablespoon butter
2 tablespoons chopped
   onion

$1/3$ cup chopped fresh
   parsley
$1/2$ teaspoon lemon zest
2 tablespoons lemon juice
Salt and freshly ground
   pepper to taste

1. Combine the zucchini and water in a microwave-safe dish. Microwave, covered, on High for 5 minutes. Drain.
2. Heat the butter in a skillet over medium heat. Sauté the onion and parsley until soft. Stir in the lemon zest and lemon juice.
3. Add the steamed zucchini to the skillet and toss. Season with salt and pepper.
4. Serve hot.

Prep Time: 5 minutes   Cook Time: 5 to 10 minutes   Yields: 4 servings

Fennel Gratin

If you haven't used fennel before, this is a great introduction to the vegetable.

2 large fennel bulbs, cut into $^1/_4$-inch slices,
   lacy tops discarded
3 tablespoons butter
$^1/_4$ cup dried bread crumbs
$^1/_4$ cup grated Parmesan cheese
2 tablespoons minced parsley
1 tablespoon fennel seeds, crushed
Salt and freshly ground pepper
2 eggs
$^1/_4$ cup milk

1. Spray an 8x8-inch glass microwave-safe baking dish with nonstick cooking spray.
2. Melt the butter in a large skillet over medium heat. Sauté the fennel in the butter for 12 to 15 minutes or until browned and almost caramelized, stirring frequently. Place in the baking dish.
3. Mix the bread crumbs, cheese, parsley, fennel seeds, salt and pepper in a bowl. Add to the fennel and mix well.
4. Beat the eggs and milk together in a bowl. Pour evenly over the fennel mixture.
5. Microwave, uncovered, on High for 8 minutes.

Prep Time: 30 minutes   Cook Time: 8 minutes   Yield: 4 servings

Rosemary Roasted New Potatoes

Rosemary and new spring potatoes are a natural pairing.

2 tablespoons olive oil
2 garlic cloves, minced
$^1/_2$ teaspoon rosemary, crushed
$^1/_2$ teaspoon thyme
$^1/_4$ teaspoon salt
$^1/_8$ teaspoon freshly ground pepper
2 pounds new potatoes, scrubbed and quartered

1. Preheat the oven to 450 degrees.
2. Mix the olive oil, garlic, rosemary, thyme, salt and pepper in a 9x13-inch baking pan. Add the potatoes and turn to coat.
3. Bake, uncovered, for about 25 minutes or until the potatoes are golden brown and tender. Turn the potatoes 2 to 3 times during baking.

Prep Time: 10 minutes   Cook Time: 25 minutes   Yield: 3 to 4 servings

Porcini Parmesan Polenta

*Creamy polenta, mushrooms, peppers, and cheese blend beautifully
in this attractive and flavorful dish.*

While many mushrooms are mild, porcini, shiitake, morel, and chanterelle mushrooms have distinct flavors and aromas that persist even after drying. To reconstitute dried mushrooms, soak in warm water for thirty minutes. Strain the soaking liquid and save it to use in a recipe, if desired. Softened mushrooms may be left whole, sliced, or chopped. Add the mushrooms at the beginning of cooking, to allow their intense flavors to permeate the dish.

2 bags (³/4 ounce each) dried porcini mushrooms
4 tablespoons butter, divided
8 ounces crimini mushrooms, sliced
1 teaspoon minced garlic
¹/2 cup dry white wine
7 cups chicken stock
2 cups cornmeal
1 cup grated Parmesan cheese, divided
Salt and freshly ground pepper to taste
Olive oil
1 red bell pepper, roasted and cut into thin strips
   (see Elk & Cherry Tartare, page 115)
¹/2 (8-ounce) fresh mozzarella ball, sliced
¹/2 cup (2 ounces) diced mozzarella cheese

1. Place the porcini mushrooms in a small bowl and cover with hot water. Set aside for 20 to 30 minutes; drain.
2. Heat 1 tablespoon butter in a large saucepan over medium heat. Sauté the crimini mushrooms in the butter until soft. Stir in the garlic. Add the wine and cook until almost dry. Add the porcini mushrooms and chicken stock and bring to a boil.
3. Whisk in the cornmeal and reduce the heat to low. Cook until the mixture is thick and pulls away from the side of the pan, stirring constantly with a wooden spoon.
4. Stir in the remaining 3 tablespoons butter, ³/4 cup Parmesan cheese, salt and pepper. Remove from the heat.
5. Preheat the oven to 350 degrees. Spray an 8x12-inch baking dish with olive oil. Spread half the polenta mixture in the baking dish. Place the bell pepper strips and mozzarella slices over the polenta. Cover with the remaining polenta mixture.
6. Top with the diced mozzarella cheese and remaining ¹/4 cup Parmesan cheese.
7. Bake for 20 to 30 minutes or until the top is golden brown.

Prep Time: 20 minutes   Soak Time: 30 minutes

Cook Time: 20 to 30 minutes   Yield: 8 to 10 servings

Whole Wheat Soda Bread

This is an easy and tasty bread. It is best eaten warm from the oven.

2 cups whole wheat flour
1 cup all-purpose flour
$1/2$ cup oats, preferably old-fashioned
3 tablespoons sugar
1 teaspoon baking powder
1 teaspoon baking soda
1 teaspoon salt
$3/4$ cup raisins (optional)
2 tablespoons canola oil
$1^3/4$ cups low-fat buttermilk

1. Preheat the oven to 350 degrees. Grease a baking sheet or 9-inch round baking pan.
2. Mix the flours, oats, sugar, baking powder, baking soda, salt and raisins in a large bowl.
3. Mix the canola oil and buttermilk in a small bowl. Add to the dry ingredients.
4. Stir to make a soft dough. Turn out onto a floured surface and knead about 10 turns.
5. Shape into a round loaf about $2^1/2$ inches thick. Place on the baking sheet.
6. Bake for 65 to 70 minutes or until a toothpick inserted in the center comes out clean.
7. Cool slightly on a wire rack before slicing.

Prep Time: 10 minutes   Cook Time: 65 to 70 minutes

Yield: 1 loaf, about 20 slices

Rhubarb Bread

This quick bread features abundant spring rhubarb.

3 cups all-purpose flour
1¹/₂ cups whole wheat flour
1 tablespoon baking soda
1¹/₂ teaspoons baking powder
1 tablespoon cinnamon
³/₄ teaspoon allspice
¹/₄ teaspoon nutmeg
4 eggs
1¹/₂ cups canola oil
2 cups packed brown sugar
1 teaspoon vanilla extract
4 cups diced rhubarb
1 cup chopped walnuts

1. Preheat the oven to 350 degrees. Grease three 5x9-inch loaf pans.
2. Mix the flours, baking soda, baking powder, cinnamon, allspice and nutmeg in a medium bowl. Set aside.
3. Combine the eggs, canola oil, brown sugar and vanilla in a large bowl. Using an electric mixer, beat until fluffy. Stir in the dry mixture just until moistened. Stir in the rhubarb and walnuts.
4. Divide the batter evenly among the pans.
5. Bake the bread for about 50 minutes or until a toothpick inserted in the center comes out clean.
6. Cool the bread in the pans for 10 to 15 minutes. Remove to a wire rack to cool completely.

Prep Time: 20 minutes   Cook Time: 50 minutes   Yield: 3 loaves

Rhubarb plants were established by early settlers and flourished in the harsh environment of the frontier. A welcome sigh of spring, these bright reddish pink stalks were so popular as pie filling, they were called "pie plants." Lacking an heirloom patch of your own, rhubarb can be found in the supermarket. Use only the stalks, as the leaves are toxic. Chopped stalks freeze well.

Lemon Cookies

These refreshing cookies are good anytime, but especially with a cup of tea.

1 cup (2 sticks) unsalted butter, softened
1 cup granulated sugar
1 egg
2 teaspoons lemon extract
1 tablespoon grated lemon zest
2 cups all-purpose flour
$^1/_2$ teaspoon salt
2 teaspoons ground ginger
Granulated sugar
1 tablespoon confectioners' sugar

1. Preheat the oven to 350 degrees.
2. Cream the butter and 1 cup granulated sugar in a large bowl with an electric mixer until fluffy. Add the egg and beat well. Mix in the lemon extract and lemon zest.
3. Combine the flour, salt and ginger in a bowl and gradually blend into the creamed mixture.
4. Roll the dough into 1-inch balls. Place about 2 to 3 inches apart on ungreased cookie sheets. Flatten slightly with a fork dipped in granulated sugar.
5. Bake for 15 minutes or until very light golden brown at the edges.
6. Remove the cookies to a wire rack and let cool. Sift the confectioners' sugar onto the cookies.

Cookie dough may be frozen for 6 months. Baked cookies also freeze well wrapped airtight.

Prep Time: 25 minutes   Cook Time: 15 minutes per batch   Yield: 36 cookies

In June 2004, Strings moved to its permanent location, Music Festival Park on the corner of Mt. Werner and Pine Grove Roads. Rain, thunder, and lightning did not dampen the enthusiasm of the community as it turned out en masse for the grand opening celebration The new facility includes a 550-seat tent, nestled in a lush garden of trees, flowers, and water features, surrounded by stunning views of the Yampa Valley and Mt. Werner. As a prelude to each performance, concertgoers gather in this serene setting, often pausing to dine or socialize with friends.

Orange Coconut Macaroons

These simple to make cookies with endless variations are a favorite with kids.

1 teaspoon grated orange zest
1 package (14 ounces) flaked coconut
1 can (14 ounces) sweetened condensed milk
2 teaspoons almond extract
1 teaspoon vanilla extract

1. Preheat the oven to 350 degrees. Line cookie sheets with parchment paper and set aside.
2. Combine the orange zest, coconut, condensed milk, almond extract and vanilla in a bowl and stir until well mixed.
3. Drop the mixture by scant tablespoonfuls onto the cookie sheets, spacing them about an inch apart.
4. Bake for 10 to 15 minutes or until light brown.
5. Place the cookie sheets on wire racks and let cool completely before removing the macaroons from the parchment paper.

Variations include: adding some miniature chocolate chips; combining lemon zest, chocolate chips, and crystallized ginger; experimenting with various extract and zest combinations.

Prep Time: 10 to 15 minutes   Cook Time: 10 to 15 minutes per batch

Yield: 3 dozen

Triple-Chocolate Nut Cookies

Irresistible, chocolaty treats, great warm with ice cream.

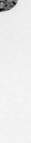

1¼ cups (2½ sticks) butter, softened
2 cups sugar
2 eggs
2 teaspoons vanilla extract
2¾ cups all-purpose flour
2 teaspoons cream of tartar
1 teaspoon baking soda
¾ cup unsweetened baking cocoa
⅛ teaspoon salt
1 cup semisweet chocolate chips
1 cup miniature chocolate chips
1 cup chopped pecans
Sugar

1. Cream the butter and sugar in a large bowl with an electric mixer until fluffy. Beat in the eggs and vanilla.
2. Mix the flour, cream of tartar, baking soda, baking cocoa and salt together and gradually blend into the creamed mixture. Stir in the chocolate chips and pecans.
3. Chill the dough for at least 1 hour or overnight.
4. Preheat the oven to 400 degrees.
5. Roll the dough into 1½-inch diameter balls and roll in sugar. Place about 2 inches apart on ungreased cookie sheets.
6. Bake for 9 to 11 minutes. Remove from the oven while slightly soft. Cool on the cookie sheets for 5 minutes, then remove to wire racks.

Prep Time: 20 minutes   Chill Time: 1 hour   Cook Time: 9 to 11 minutes per batch

Yield: 6 dozen

Springtime Cheesecake

CHEESECAKE
1/2 cup graham cracker
  crumbs
2 tablespoons butter, melted
3 packages (8 ounces each)
  low-fat cream cheese,
  softened
1 cup sugar
3 eggs, at room temperature
3/4 cup reduced-fat sour
  cream
1/2 teaspoon grated orange
  zest
1 tablespoon orange juice

BERRY GLAZE
1/4 cup sugar
2 teaspoons cornstarch

1 cup strawberries,
  blueberries or raspberries,
  mashed
1/4 cup water

CHOCOLATE GLAZE
3 ounces semisweet baking
  chocolate
2 tablespoons unsalted
  butter
1 tablespoon corn syrup
1/2 teaspoon vanilla extract

GARNISH
Mint
2 cups fresh berries

FOR THE CHEESECAKE:

1. Preheat the oven to 350 degrees. Coat an 8-inch springform pan with nonstick cooking spray. Place the graham cracker crumbs in a bowl, add the melted butter and stir to mix. Press firmly onto the bottom of the pan.

2. Beat the cream cheese and sugar in a large bowl with an electric mixer at medium speed until smooth. Beat in the eggs one at a time until blended. Beat in the sour cream, orange zest and orange juice. Pour over the crust.

3. Bake for 45 minutes or until the edge of the cheesecake puffs slightly and the center still jiggles slightly when shaken. Turn off the oven and leave the door closed. Let the cheesecake cool in the closed oven for 1 hour. Carefully run a thin knife around the edge of the pan to release the cheesecake. Cool in the pan on a wire rack.

4. Remove the pan side and place the cheesecake on a serving plate. Spread with your choice of glaze and garnish with mint and berries. Serve at room temperature.

FOR THE BERRY GLAZE:

Combine the ingredients in a saucepan. Bring to a boil; reduce the heat. Simmer for 7 minutes, stirring constantly. If using raspberries, strain through a sieve to remove the seeds. Let stand until warm. Stir before using.

FOR THE CHOCOLATE GLAZE:

Heat the chocolate, butter, corn syrup and vanilla in a saucepan over low heat, stirring until smooth. Remove from the heat and let cool slightly.

Prep Time: 20 to 25 minutes   Cook Time: 45 minutes   Cool Time: 1 hour

Yield: 8 to 10 servings

Kahlúa Swirl Cake

2 cups all-purpose flour
³/4 teaspoon baking powder
³/4 teaspoon baking soda
³/4 teaspoon salt
³/4 teaspoon mace, divided
¹/2 cup (1 stick) butter,
  softened
1 cup sugar
2 eggs
1 teaspoon vanilla extract
³/4 cup sour cream

³/4 cup plus 3 tablespoons
  Kahlúa, divided
¹/3 cup packed brown sugar
¹/3 cup chopped pecans
¹/4 teaspoon cinnamon
³/4 cup confectioners' sugar
2 tablespoons butter,
  softened
Pecan halves (optional)

1. Preheat the oven to 350 degrees. Grease and flour a bundt cake pan.
2. Combine the flour, baking powder, baking soda, salt and ¹/2 teaspoon mace.
3. Beat the butter, sugar, eggs and vanilla in a large bowl with an electric mixer. Add the dry ingredients, sour cream and ³/4 cup Kahlúa alternately to the butter mixture.
4. Combine the brown sugar, pecans, cinnamon and the remaining ¹/4 teaspoon mace in a small bowl.
5. Layer ¹/3 of the cake batter, ¹/2 of the streusel filling, ¹/3 of the cake batter, the remaining streusel filling and remaining cake batter.
6. Bake on a low oven rack for 45 minutes.
7. Remove from the oven and let cool for 10 minutes. Invert onto a rack to cool completely. Remove from the pan.
8. Combine the confectioners' sugar, butter and the remaining 3 tablespoons Kahlúa in a bowl and mix until smooth, adding water if needed for glaze consistency. Spoon the glaze over the cake, letting some drip down the side.
9. Top with pecan halves.

For low altitude, use 1 teaspoon baking powder, 1¹/4 cups sugar, and 1 cup sour cream.

Prep Time: 30 minutes   Cook Time: 45 minutes   Yield: 16 to 20 servings

Winter flows right into spring, literally. With an average of over 300 inches of snowfall every winter, spring runoff in the Yampa River is deafening and beckons kayakers from all over Colorado to our paddling playground. Flow reports replace snow reports, and the car roofs trade their skis for brightly colored boats. The Yampa River swells, often overtaking its banks, daring paddlers to take it on. In June, the annual Yampa River Festival is hosted with kayak racing, slalom, and rodeo events, not to mention the Crazy River Dog contest.

Rhubarb Pie

A treasured heirloom recipe.

Pastry for 1 double-crust 9-inch pie
1 cup sugar
2 tablespoons all-purpose flour
$^1/_8$ teaspoon salt
2 eggs, beaten
4 cups rhubarb, cut into $^1/_2$-inch pieces
    (about 6 large stalks)
2 tablespoons cold butter, cut into small pieces
1 tablespoon milk
1 tablespoon sugar

1. Preheat the oven to 450 degrees.
2. Divide the pastry into halves. Roll the first half into an 11-inch circle on a lightly floured surface and line a 9-inch pie plate. Reserve the second half for the top crust.
3. Mix the sugar, flour and salt in a large bowl. Add the eggs and rhubarb and mix well. Pour the rhubarb mixture into the pie shell and dot with the butter.
4. Roll the reserved pastry into an 11-inch circle on the floured surface. Moisten the exposed edge of the bottom pastry with water, using a pastry brush. Place the second circle of dough on top of the rhubarb. Seal the edges and tuck under. Flute to form a neat edge and tight seal. Cut six 1-inch slits in the top near the center of the pie. Brush the top with the milk and sprinkle with the sugar.
5. Bake for 10 minutes; reduce the oven temperature to 350 degrees. Bake for 55 to 65 minutes longer or until the top is golden brown. You may need to cover the edge of the pastry with foil to prevent overbrowning. Place a baking sheet or pizza pan under the pie to catch any juices that may run out and burn.

For low altitude, reduce cooking time by ten minutes.

Prep Time: 10 to 20 minutes   Cook Time: 65 to 75 minutes
Yield: 6 to 8 servings

Strawberry Pie with Fruit Glaze

This versatile recipe can be tailored to suit your whim. The rhubarb glaze imparts an invigorating, slightly tart taste, while the strawberry glaze provides a burst of flavor.

RHUBARB GLAZE
$^1/_2$ cup strawberries, cleaned, hulled and chopped
1 cup finely chopped rhubarb (about 2 large stalks)
$^1/_4$ cup water
1 cup sugar
$1^1/_2$ tablespoons cornstarch
Pinch of salt
1 tablespoon butter

STRAWBERRY GLAZE
2 cups strawberries, cleaned and hulled
$^1/_2$ cup water
1 cup sugar
2 tablespoons cornstarch
$^1/_8$ teaspoon salt

PIE
1 baked (9-inch) pie shell
4 cups strawberries, cleaned and hulled
Sweetened whipped cream

Prepare the rhubarb or strawberry glaze.

FOR THE RHUBARB GLAZE:
Combine the chopped strawberries, rhubarb and water in a small saucepan. Cook over medium heat for 10 minutes or until rhubarb is tender, stirring frequently. Mix the sugar, cornstarch and salt in a small bowl and add to the fruit mixture. Cook for 2 to 3 minutes longer or until the sauce has thickened. Add the butter. Remove from the heat and stir until the butter is melted and blended in. Cool for 10 to15 minutes.

FOR THE STRAWBERRY GLAZE:
Bring the strawberries and water to a boil in a saucepan and cook for 2 to 3 minutes. Strain; reserve the juice and discard the solids. Mix the sugar, cornstarch and salt in a small bowl and add to the reserved juice. Bring to a boil, stirring constantly. Cook until the mixture is thick, stirring constantly. Remove from the heat and cool for 10 to15 minutes.

FOR THE PIE:
1. Fill the pie shell with the strawberries.
2. Spoon the glaze of choice over the strawberries in the pie shell, glazing each berry and letting the sauce fill in the gaps between the berries.
3. Chill in the refrigerator for at least 2 hours or until the glaze is set.
4. Remove from the refrigerator about 30 minutes before serving. Serve with sweetened whipped cream.

Prep Time: 45 to 50 minutes   Cook Time: 10 to 15 minutes

Chill Time: 2 hours   Yield: 6 to 8 servings

Chocolate Mousse

The epitome of simplicity and elegance, this dessert can be made a few days ahead. Whip the cream just before serving.

1 package (8 ounces) semisweet baking chocolate
$1/4$ cup water
5 eggs, separated
1 teaspoon vanilla extract
Cinnamon Whipped Cream (see recipe below)

1. Melt the chocolate with the water in a double boiler, stirring until the chocolate is smooth and glossy. Remove from the heat.
2. Beat in the egg yolks one at a time. Stir in the vanilla.
3. Beat the egg whites until stiff peaks form and fold into the chocolate mixture.
4. Divide the mousse equally among 8 stemmed glasses. Cover with plastic wrap and chill in the refrigerator for at least 6 hours or up to 4 days.
5. Serve with Cinnamon Whipped Cream.

Prep Time: 15 minutes   Chill Time: 6 hours   Yield: 8 servings

Cinnamon Whipped Cream

$1/2$ pint (1 cup) chilled heavy whipping cream
2 tablespoons confectioners' sugar
$1/4$ teaspoon cinnamon

1. Whip the cream at medium-high speed with an electric mixer until the cream begins to thicken.
2. Gradually add the sugar and cinnamon and continue beating until soft peaks form. Do not overbeat.

♪ To obtain maximum volume, have the bowl, beaters, and cream well chilled.

Frozen Orange Chocolate Soufflé

The Snowbird restaurant, located slopeside in the Ptarmigan Inn, allows people to dine while they watch the skiers go by. Their Frozen Orange Chocolate Soufflé was the First Place People's Choice Award winner for the 2003 Decadent Desserts fund-raiser.

CHEF CHUCK BELL

6 egg yolks
1/4 cup sugar
2 3/4 cups whipping cream
2 tablespoons Grand Marnier or other orange liqueur
2 tablespoons light cacao liqueur
2 ounces white chocolate, melted
1/4 cup orange juice
18 large orange shells, cleaned
Sweetened whipped cream and shaved dark
   chocolate for garnish

1. Beat the egg yolks and sugar in a large bowl with an electric mixer until pale yellow and thick.
2. Whip the cream until stiff peaks form in a bowl with an electric mixer. Fold into the egg mixture.
3. Fold the Grand Marnier, cacao, chocolate and orange juice into the egg mixture.
4. Fill the orange shells with the soufflé mixture and freeze for 24 hours
5. Serve with sweetened whipped cream and shaved dark chocolate.

♪ If you are concerned about using raw egg yolks, use yolks from eggs pasteurized in their shells, which are sold at some specialty food stores, or use an equivalent amount of pasteurized egg substitute.

Prep Time: 25 minutes   Freeze Time: 24 hours   Yield: 18 servings

The annual High Country Garden Tour is the premier summer fund-raising event sponsored by the Guild of Strings in the Mountains. On this day, selected Steamboat homeowners open their remarkable gardens for the Tour. As locals and visitors stroll through the various gardens, Master Gardeners are on hand to answer questions. Adding to the charm of this lovely day, festival and local musicians perform at various locations

Contributors

Thanks to all who contributed and tested recipes, those who offered their
writing expertise and advice, and those whom we may have inadvertently omitted.
Special thanks to our families for their patience and support.

Liz Aldendifer	Natalie Cowan	Roberta Geier
Pat Aljanich	Jane Davis	Dave Glantz
Philamena Baird	Annie DeGroff	Don Grant
Harriet Barberi	Elaine Dermody	Marsha Grant
Lucelia Belisle	Alison Dougan	Ellen Grapin
Sandy Berger	Sue Dreska	Betse Grassby
Sylvia Boss	Janet Dring	Denise Greig
Gloria Bradfield	Dasha Durian	Tina Greig
Jane Carpenter	Michael Durian	Lynne Grimsley
Sue Carpenter	Bill Emerson	Patty Grossman
Kay Clagett	Judith Emerson	Bill Hamilton
Carole Cohen	Andrea Erickson	Dori Hamilton
Paula Collins	Claire Faler	Linda Jensen Hamlet
Hope Cook	Monica Fenton	Jane Hannon
Lorna Cook	Linda Fisher-Faiola	Jan Hardy
Susan Coover	Edie Fogliano	John Hatch
Bev Cowan	Bernadette Foy	Marianne Hickey

Contributors

Barbara Hilf	Marilyn Mastoras	Tosia Sauter
Starlett Hollingsworth	Danna McDonough	Ann Scolnick
Ann Hooe	Michael McFarlane	Emily Seaver
Donna Howell	Patti McFarlane	Annamarie Shunny
Gloria James	Bonnie McGee	Gloria Smith
Evzena Kellner Jameson	Lois McKown	Susan Sonnenschein
Charlotte Jensen	Suzi Mitchell	Tibby Speare
Margot Johns	Jane Morris	Sandy St. Clair
Judy Jones	Holly Nelson	Barbara Stofan
Mary Lou Jones	Kitty Nolin	Paula Tissot
Millie Judson	Gail Overgaard	Diane Trabulsi
Nancy Kramer	Jody Patten	Karen Tucker
Kathleen Laterzo	Marit Perkins	Karen Vanderwall
Joanne Lathrop	Louise Poppen	Mary Vanderwall
Ute Lichtenstein	Debbie Ratliff	Kathy Vaynkof
Elaine Love	Richard Reed	Jeanelle Waldrop
Kay Makens	Cindy Richmond	Diane Wallace
Piilani Cook Mason	Jean Ryland	Sandra Worthen

Thanks

Thanks to the following restaurants and chefs for sharing their special recipes with us.

A Catered Affair
Chef - Marcee Marie

Mazzola's
Cooper & Tracy Barnett

Antares
Chef - Rocky Lebrun

Old West Steakhouse
Don Silva

Blue Bonnet Catering
Chef - Melissa Cartan

Riggio's
Chef - Dominick Riggio

Café Diva
Chef - Kate Van Rensselaer

Sheraton Steamboat Resort
Chef - Scott M. King

Catamount Ranch & Club
Chef - Sam Gordon

Snowbird
Chef - Chuck Bell

Cottonwood Grill
Chefs - Peter Lautner & Michael Fragola

The Home Ranch
Chef - Clyde Nelson

Freshies
Chef - Greg Margolis

Tobiano
Chef - Richie Billingham

Giovanni's
Dave & Jennifer Sypert

Tugboat Grill & Pub
Chef - Kenyon Coxon

La Montaña
Chef - Damon Renfroe

Chef - David Nelson

Marnos Custom Catering
Chef - Nanny Marno

Chef - Jacques Wilson

Thanks to the following musicians for their recipes and stories.

Paul Eachus • Ilya Kaler • Olga Kaler • Cary Lewis
Lambert Orkis • Gene Pokorny • Ralph Votapek

Index

Index

Index

Index

Steamboat Seasons

A MEDLEY OF RECIPES

Strings in the Mountains
Cookbook

P.O. Box 774627

Steamboat Springs, Colorado

80477

Telephone: (970) 879-5056

Extension 110

Fax: (970) 879-7460

Website:

www.stringsinthemountains.com

YOUR ORDER	QTY	TOTAL
Steamboat Seasons at $24.95 per book		$
Colorado residents add sales tax*		$
Shipping & handling at $4.95 for first book; $2.00 for each additional book shipped to the same address**		$
	TOTAL	$

METHOD OF PAYMENT: [   ] American Express   [   ] MasterCard   [   ] VISA

[   ] Check payable to Strings in the Mountains Cookbook

Account Number _____ Exp. Date _____

Signature _____

SOLD TO: (*please print*)

Name _____

Address _____

City _____ State _____ Zip _____

Daytime Phone _____ Evening Phone _____

Fax _____ E-mail _____

SHIP TO: (*attach list if additional shipping addresses*)

Name _____

Address _____

City _____ State _____ Zip _____

Photocopies will be accepted.

*If order is shipped or picked up within the City of Steamboat Springs, add 8.4%; if order is shipped within Routt County, add 3.9%; if order is shipped within the State of Colorado, add 2.9%. **Call for quote for international shipping.